7626

792.
02
You

Young, John
Directing the play from
    selection to opening night

DIRECTING THE PLAY

DIRECTING
THE PLAY

From Selection to Opening Night

BY

JOHN WRAY YOUNG

KENNIKAT PRESS
Port Washington, N. Y./London

DIRECTING THE PLAY

Copyright © 1958 by John Wray Young
Reissued in 1972 by Kennikat Press by arrangement
Library of Congress Catalog Card No: 74-161024
ISBN 0-8046-1541-1

Manufactured by Taylor Publishing Company   Dallas, Texas

For Margaret Mary Young II
and John Wray Young III—
better known to me as
Jock and Jill

CONTENTS

PROLOGUE

Directing, as a formal element in theatre, is new. I use the adjective advisedly, choosing to regard theatre as a continuous art form which has retained certain basic principles and purposes established twenty-five centuries ago in ancient Greece.

The director's entrance so late in the story of theatre explains the relative paucity of writings about his function and his methods. Certainly volumes on the playwright, the actor, and the designer are much more numerous on library shelves. Even the other newcomer, the lighting expert, finds many excellent books waiting for his perusal.

We may explain this seeming neglect of the director if we recognize that the very title has lacked precise definition and that the new overall form of theatre in the United States has not tended to clarify an understanding of it.

Our colleagues in Europe come much closer to knowing and respecting the directorial concept in modern theatre. This has not been too difficult for them, since several of the giants of the European theatre have been directors, able to write effectively of what they knew and what they did.

Stanislavsky, Boleslavsky, and the others who were able to translate their life in art to readable words, have left a vital legacy to those who want the broad concept of the artist-director. This has been gratifying to the student of theatre, but it is not enough for the practitioner.

In modern England, which has but one full-fledged theatre department in its higher educational system, this lack of practical writing on direction presents little problem. With the soundly established repertory system, the young English director learns in the same apprentice, on-the-job method of the commercial theatre which for so long was the actors' sole training ground in America.

Today more than seventeen hundred colleges and universities in our land have courses in theatre. And an undefinable number—estimated from 10,000 to 150,000—of community groups regularly produce plays at various levels of competence. This amazing growth of the noncommercial theatre in the United States has, naturally, brought forth a large amount of writing; but lacking, as I have said, is a proportionate amount on the central issue of directing the play.

But as the director began to exert an ever increasing influence on the play form, writings did start to appear in this country. I recall the thrill which came to the Youngs in 1930. We were students at the University of Iowa when we learned that John Dolman was coming to Iowa City. His book, *The Art of Play Production,* had just appeared, and we hastily merged enough of our skimpy student funds to purchase a copy. Mr. Dolman did arrive, gave an excellent lecture, and autographed our copy of his book. It still holds a proud place among the many autographed volumes on our shelves, for we felt, and many agree, that this was the first significant work on the new concept of directorial procedure to be published in this country.

Many years later, in 1949, Mr. Dolman gave the theatre another splendid volume, *The Art of Acting.* This fine gentleman left in his books an important contribution to the total of im-

portant works on theatre. They reflect his fine theatrical heritage
and his high concept of theatre as an art form.

There have been other books and chapters in books concerned
with the director in modern theatre practice. However, most of
the writing has treated theory rather than practice. Some au-
thors tend to think of the director as a superman, interesting
to think of but rarely found in the flesh. If we could limit use
of the title to those few who fit this glorified definition, we
might need no more books. If theatre were confined to the
rarefied atmosphere of Robert Edmond Jones' *The Dramatic
Imagination,* perhaps we could be content with Stanislavsky,
Boleslavsky, and their mighty colleagues.

As we move through the second half of the twentieth century, such a comfortable limitation of the director is no longer
possible. Someone holds that title in each of the tens of thousands of productions produced each year by the American noncommercial theatre. For them, philosophy is not enough. They
want to be helped.

This wide need became apparent when the reviews of my first
book, *The Community Theatre and How It Works,* came in
from about the country. Letters began to come in from makers
of theatre. Their substance was: "You have told us how to or-
ganize and manage a community theatre. Now tell us, in a practical way, how we can direct our plays to make them better.
After all, the play is the reason for all the rest."

This book is written to fill that expressed need. The experience of writing it has brought a number of discoveries. First,
despite the writing thus far on the subject, there has been a
widespread tendency among the best directors to keep their
techniques to themselves. Most of the men and women who are
experts in play direction work under the closed rehearsal system, a necessary rule if efficiency is to be considered. Obviously

students of directing could not get far trying to enter those closed stage doors.

I looked next at the courses in directing at our leading universities. Here there seemed to be two principal tendencies: to ask the student to spend too much time with the philosophy of directing, or asking him to "direct" without a clear pattern of procedure.

It is rare when the undergraduate, or even the M. A. candidate, is capable of translating the highest profound theories about direction into practical action. It seems to me that only after some years in the field can one begin to understand and appreciate the full meaning of a work such as *The Dramatic Imagination*. This is not to say that the college student should not read it. He should absorb as much of it as possible, but I fear he may not find much in the way of fundamental technique for the job of learning how to direct.

The second practice is to ask university students to direct a series of short plays or scenes on their own. If the teacher-director can follow through each rehearsal with the student, explain each step of technique, and give constructive criticism after each rehearsal, then the learning-by-directing method is fine. It requires, however, that the teacher devote full course-time to one student. This is impossible, and many good courses in directing use the work of one student as example for the rest of the class.

This is better, but not enough. If we grant, as we do, that directing is an individual art form, or technique, or craft, then we realize that it is the *individual* talent which needs developing and training. The analogy of the master piano class, as compared with the single student and the master, is perhaps applicable. The observers at the master class may get inspiration and some practical help, but it is probably less than they would receive had they the master's undivided attention.

The teaching of directing, then, presents special problems in a field which already has its share. The magnitude of the job is apparent if we keep in mind the vast number of productions in the noncommercial theatre, and realize that, in most cases, those engaged in direction as volunteers will probably never be able to return to a campus for formal instruction. Some of them have become expert by self-teaching and learning on the job. Yet even they have wanted a logical, progressive guide through the procedure of play directing.

Directing the Play from Selection to Opening Night is that guide. It is based upon the experience of two hundred productions, and is planned to give directors, at various stages of development, a blueprint of technique. Much of it is designed to be taught to each company the director will meet. The understanding and practice of fundamentals will make good actors better, beginning players passable.

I believe the book will also interest that constantly increasing number of Americans who want to know more about the cultural phenomenon of the burgeoning noncommercial theatre in the United States.

Finally, the book is written with deep regard for the discipline of theatre, that factor so rarely understood, too often neglected. It seems to me that theatre is most commonly humiliated by those who do not recognize that it has a demanding discipline, worthy of the dignity of other high professions. Too often, young people look at theatre and say, "I'd like to be an actor, a director, a playwright."

This is not wrong, but we must remember that theatre is a difficult, demanding profession. It is this very difficulty which has challenged the imagination of Americans and made them want to do community theatre and do it well. The generally high level of noncommercial theatre is constant testimony to the quality of teaching in the educational theatre, and to the self-teaching in many community theatres.

In 1958, however, I think we would agree that of all the areas of theatre, the directorial most needs assistance. Only a fraction of our community theatres can yet afford full-time professional direction. A not much larger percentage of the 25,000 high schools doing plays have the services of a completely trained director.

For those thousands of persons who are asked to accomplish the intricate and specialized task of guiding a play from the first reading of the text to opening night, it is my sincere wish that this book will be of service.

JOHN WRAY YOUNG

March 1958

DIRECTING THE PLAY

CHAPTER ONE

The Director Prepares the Play

T HERE is a fine spirit of adventure about the entire process of theatre. It is a part of that magnetic appeal which has caused those of talent through the ages to work at the hard tasks of writing, acting, and producing living theatre. In a very real sense its magic has radiated out from those who work in theatre and brought into playhouses of various forms those who would share the experience of the play as audience.

At various times, the sharp impact of a single genius has been at the center of the attraction of theatre; more often, there has been a collective result of a group of sincere, often capable, persons who rehearsed and prepared a play for those who might come to enjoy.

The ebb and flow of dramatic activity through the centuries follows closely the presence or absence of great playwrights or great actors. In a few happy decades the two types of talent have been present simultaneously, making theatre of memorable stature.

As we shall see, the director, as a part of theatre, came late upon the scene, hardly identifiable until the twentieth century. Of the early examples there are many colorful stories, but perhaps none left richer legends that David Belasco. With or without the clerical collar, he achieved such impressive points with his productions that he helped to make the director an accepted factor in modern play production.

Among the legends about Belasco, who lived from 1854 to 1931, is one which recalls his own special flair for getting what he wanted from his players. In early rehearsals of one play, he pointedly referred to his elaborate gold watch, making certain that his leading actress knew full well the story of its great sentimental and monetary value.

Many rehearsals later, Belasco came to an impasse with his star. She could not reach a certain emotional peak he wanted. Time after time they did the scene. At last, with tensions stretched to the utmost, the great man stopped the rehearsal with a shouted "No! No! That's not it!" Then, in apparent fury, he grabbed the precious watch from his pocket and smashed it to the stage floor at the feet of his star. She had barely time to see the irreplaceable treasure scatter into a thousand pieces when, with a shake of his white mane, Belasco spoke into her horrified eyes, "*Now*, do the scene!"

Needless to say, the emotional peak was reached and added another high point to the production. Long afterward the star learned that Belasco kept a large stock of cheap watches for breaking!

Today, most leading directors tend to be skilled artists who work with poise and self-control. There may be exceptions, but most of the men and women who direct the finest productions have the dignity and inspiration essential to fine leadership. Skilled in all phases of play production, the director is the catalyst, chiefly responsible for turning the dross of scenery, light, some printed words, and a group of emotionally charged human beings into the gold of theatre experience.

Where has he come from? We know that during theatre's

long centuries, there have been those who said, or suggested, or argued, about the way things should be done. It is likely that Thespis, after that first leap from the crowd, buoyed by the sense of importance which came to the first actor to speak alone, began to give advice in directorial fashion.

Later, in the theatre of Athens, both the poet and the choragus may have been vocal about production details. After all, they both wanted to be crowned with ivy. At this distance, it is intriguing to wonder which won the most arguments: the man who wrote the play or the man who furnished the money? There have been modern versions of this pair.

Still further along, we find a playwright who sensed so completely that plays need direction that he wrote many of the basic guides into his lines. The most cursory student of Shakespeare knows how far he went in writing direction into his verse. It may be this noble tradition which has led some modern playwrights to attempt direction of their own works. When they are both directors *and* playwrights, it has worked very well. There have been cases when the direction should have been given to a director.

The evolution of this new artist continued after Shakespeare. In varying degrees, the managers, the producer-managers, and the stage managers had something to say about how things should be done. However, there was little conscious understanding of the responsibilities and rights of a true director. Seventy years ago, in an argument between star and stage manager, the star won automatically, for it was the star talents which brought people to the American theatre in the nineteenth century.

There were a few American plays in that period which could stand as their own drawing cards no matter who played them, but much of that era of American drama seems most inadequate today, as you may reaffirm in an hour at the library.

Through the eighteenth and nineteenth centuries, while there was growing evidence of the need for a central mind in the production of a play, it was Shakespeare who exerted the most consistent influence. This came in the form of "inherited business" —the details of which were passed from generation to generation by actors, actor-managers, and stage managers. This tradition that there was a best way to read a line, do a gesture, or play a scene seems an interesting foreshadowing of the day when the director would emerge on the stages of the world.

It is pleasant that the first general acknowledgment of the director came with the rise of the European art theatre, and a bit later in the community theatre in the United States. Certainly Antoine, Stanislavsky, Meyerhold, and the others were the inspiration for Sam Hume, Maurice Browne, Gilmor Brown, and Fred McConnell. That these pioneers found in a volunteer theatre the finest soil for the growth of the ideals of the European art theatre accelerated the acceptance of the director as a major theatre artist.

Working often with simple facilities, and with players who at times held no more firm background in theatre than their membership cards in the Drama League, it was necessary that the director assume full responsibility for, and control of, the multitudinous details of production. The frequent artistic triumphs of the first little theatres may have helped the commercial theatre to see that a director was an essential—not merely a convenience at such times as a Belasco happened along.

In the last fifty years the director has developed as a theatre artist to the point where his capabilities often determine the success or failure of a production. Particularly is this true in the community theatre of America, which faces its enormous development with a continuous shortage of properly trained directors.

Yet we know that many of the finest directors of the commercial theatre have been self-taught, or at best, trained through
a sort of on-the-job apprentice system. We also see many community theatres with splendid records, whose volunteer directors
have achieved their skills in somewhat the same fashion. The
educational theatre, occupied first with training teachers and
second in developing the infrequent young talents which may
be strong enough to face the battle of the commercial theatre,
have thus far made the training of community theatre leadership a very poor third.

Since it may be a considerable time before the objectives are
reversed, and since community theatre production continues to
grow in quantity, it is our concern to discuss principles and
methods which, proven by time, may assist directors of experience, and educate to some extent those who would like to serve
theatre from the directorial chair.

Although directors are often unjustly accused for a playwright's faults, it is obvious that except in the first production
of a new script, the director's work begins with the selection of
the play. Unfortunately this is not only a difficult decision but
one which exerts a dominant influence all the way to the fall of
the curtain on the last performance.

There are various methods used in community theatre play
selection but it is not the means which need concern us so much
as the result. A beginning overall statement may well be that
no director should be asked to produce a play he does not care
for, and that a director ought not be allowed to do a play which
is unsuitable for his audience.

The first premise implies that a director needs a broad cultural appetite, especially if he is to do two or more plays a
season. We have heard of individuals who direct only comedy
or melodrama or tragedy. A community group with a staff of

directors might be able to divide types to fit personal idiosyncrasies, but this is a form of specialization we hardly need if a theatre and its program are to have balance.

The second premise implies that some plays are unsuitable for some audiences. The unsuitability of a dramatic work depends on factors ranging from morals and profanity to a particular town's aversion to certain subject matter or a certain play type. I know of one city where fantasy, no matter how well done, is death to the box office.

However, these factors are generally well considered in the common practice of director and playreading committee working together, with final approval of play selection by the organization's board of directors. One of the more tantalizing truths of theatre is that *nothing* can guarantee the success of a play, or insure its warm acceptance when the opening night arrives. We can, however, avoid many pitfalls which increase the precariousness of production.

Certainly no single factor tends to have more bearing on the end result than the *quality* of a play. If the work of the playwright is good, the chances of success increase. I can already hear a thousand voices asking, "Why, then, have there been so many horrible Shakespearean productions?" It may be that not many of our volunteer players have the speech and the background for the assignment; and few modern directors possess the training and skill for successfully re-creating Elizabethan drama. That it can be done, and splendidly, even with young people of college age, will be attested by anyone who has seen a B. Iden Payne production at the University of Texas in recent years.

Noncommercial players in community situations seem to do better with contemporary drama, and a sound manuscript is at least an augury of success. In support, I might mention that I do not recall ever hearing of a production of *Harvey* so bad that it failed.

Today we spend a great deal of our listening, viewing, and reading time in absorbing pronouncements about the importance of quality. It affects our choice of soap flakes, automobiles, and cigarettes. It is a fine American characteristic to want the best quality for our money. Yet how often have we seen the intricate, demanding procedure of play production begin with the central factor, the play, obviously of poor value. This is, sadly enough, most often true in secondary schools where many other elements are lacking and difficult. The excuse, stated perhaps thousands of times a year, is "We can't afford any, or more, royalty."

In view of all we know this is really thespic blasphemy. I don't know of a high school which would ask its band to play with impossible instruments, or its teams to take the field in less than the best equipment that could be afforded; yet how often the high school director announces tryouts for a play which has as its sole appeal a royalty price-tag of five or ten dollars.

For years, many of us have said "Royalty is the best money you spend," but it needs endless repetition. Of course there are many fifty-dollar royalty plays not worth doing, but the confidence of a broker in setting the higher price does have a general relation to quality.

In many areas of the amateur theatre it is not widely known that the leading playbrokers, who tend to control the best material, are very fair in adjusting royalty quotations to fit specific problems. Unfortunately, they are often victimized by untruths as to seating capacities, admission charges, and other economic details.

Certainly if the project is honestly an attempt to produce a play worth an admission price, enough of the income ought to be earmarked to buy the rights to the best possible manuscript. If the real purpose is simply to raise money for band uniforms or football blankets, then I beg you, hold a bazaar, give a minstrel show, but do not prostitute the name of theatre.

A further sobering thought for the director is that the poorer the quality of the play, the more will be demanded from *him* in transforming it into an evening of value.

In considering quality, we do not take the number of Broadway performances to be analogous to the karat system in evaluating gold. There have been many plays presented around Times Square and marked as "failures" because they did not reach the one hundred performance mark, which have gone on to long and profitable careers in community theatre. One day these plays may *begin* their careers before the right audiences, but so long as our best playwrights insist on putting their work through the treadmill of Broadway, the community theatre will have to continue to sift each season's "failures" for usable material.

What then is the director's initial concern as he begins to read suitable and available manuscripts? To me, opening the cover of a new play has always been a special and stimulating adventure. As the imaginary curtain rises, I sit back, relax, and prepare for enjoyment. It is a close copy of what I do when I take my place in the orchestra before the performance of an actual play. It is going to the theatre of imagination.

The first reading of a play ought to find the director regarding the experience exactly like an audience of one. There should be no concern about casting, scenic problems, or any of the actual factors of production. The play should flow freely from the pages in a special private performance. If it brings laughter or tears, so much the better. Such emotional power from mere words speaks loudly for what may happen when the black type is transmuted into human, breathing life. The director is seeking a theatre experience, and if he finds it, then he can move to other considerations.

This finding a reflection of theatre experience in silent reading is not easy; years of practice help most, yet I feel it is the soundest way to search for material which has meaning for the director. Of course, seeing an actual performance is easier, provided the director-as-audience does not succumb to the magic of a great acting talent or two, which may give a surface glow to a play which may later prove to be inferior.

This separation of play and star has always been a problem for the critics. Often we have read their writings to the effect that a certain play had little value except as "played by so-and-so." It is important in community theatre to find the truth of these "players over play" reviews. When *The Great Sebastians* opened in New York we read that no one but the Lunts could ever make it much of a success. When I read the manuscript, however, I had a delightful hour and a half in "theatre of imagination." My wife, Margaret Mary, and I proceeded to learn the roles and the company went into rehearsal for a December opening at the Shreveport Playhouse. We found what Howard Lindsay and Russel Crouse had known all along. *The Great Sebastians* is a delightful play, destined for success in the noncommercial theatre.

Since this elimination of the star as a factor touches the whole matter of play selection for the noncommercial theatre, it is well for the director to follow the viewing of a commercial production with a careful reading of the manuscript. Though it is hard to do after the experience of the produced play, he ought to try in this reading to seek a new emotional experience. If the comedy lines seem drab, if emotional peaks leave him unmoved, then perhaps it was the *players* and not the *play* which had real theatrical valué.

But once the play has pleased the director-as-audience, either with or without viewing an actual production, attention has now to be given to considering the potential response of the actual future audience. Beginning directors may think that this problem diminishes for directors who have come to know their audiences intimately through years of production in the same playhouse. As one now beginning a third decade in the same theatre, I grant that certain facts can be learned about audiences, but most of these facts seem negative. I can tell you more about the types of plays which Shreveport Little Theatre audiences do not like than I can foretell exactly what will please them.

A few seasons back, we decided that we could no longer delay doing *The Cocktail Party,* though none of us hoped for more than a succes d'estime. I had written and spoken frequently about the gradual rise in audience ability through the years. In the case of Eliot's splendid work, however, I was certain we were asking too much of them. It was with pleased surprise, then, that we saw *The Cocktail Party* become a popular success for us.

Audiences are intriguing, as subject to whims and fancies as the individuals of which they are composed. After *The Cocktail Party* it seemed obvious that a delightfully intelligent play like *The Chalk Garden* would be their dish. Although we gave it a handsome production with an excellent company, many of our public found the play had little for them!

Estimating audience capabilities and attitudes, while a necessary factor in play selection, will never become an exact science. If it were possible to devise a pattern of such measurement, some brilliant fellow would already have figured it out and would be earning a million dollars a year as a Forecaster of Audience Reactions.

The safest course, and the objective in noncommercial theatre production aimed at continuance through season after season, is not to tempt audience disapproval by venturing too far from the apparent general level of understanding. This will vary from one community to another, being colored by everything from average educational backgrounds to the dominant employment groups of the town. It is well known that the average American audience prefers to laugh, and perhaps it is this vast consumption of comic ideas and plots which makes a good comedy suitable for community theatre production perhaps the rarest form of current writing. Each year we witness the rise and fall of comedians on television, although a great deal of money and the finest talents are devoted to maintaining their Trendex positions. The example of Perry Como paying Goodman Ace $9,000 a week to write a few amusing lines for a once-a-week program indicates the current high market value of laughter.

So in most situations, the director will have to accept the fact that even if he can find enough comedies for half his season's program, he will be apt to hear complaints from some of his audience about the other plays. It is an old problem and a current one, likely to be with us so long as we are a nation which likes to laugh. The real objective, the ultimate goal for any theatre, is to develop in its audiences the habit and desire for *playgoing* as opposed to seeing a particular play.

As the director moves on toward decision, he considers the potentials of his players. This problem is different for the educational theatre since casting there begins with the premise that all the players are within a narrow age group. Occasionally in community theatre it is necessary to put young players in older roles, but generally there is a wide age range in the acting company.

Perhaps a more important factor for the director is the general level of experience and background. A young community theatre is not apt to have players with enough seasoning to do well in Greek tragedy, Shakespeare, or Restoration comedy. The college and university are more free to choose from the finest works of classic drama. After all, in most situations it is the educational values which come first in their programs. There are, of course, town-and-gown situations where the major emphasis has to be on entertainment, but they are in the minority. Certainly the college years are the time for young people, both as players and audience, to have the privilege of coming to know the masterpieces of pre-twentieth century theatre.

There are numerical considerations for the director as he ponders the decision about the next play. There may be some, but not many, organizations with sufficient manpower to do *Mister Roberts* and *Stalag 17* in succession. Of course, the director who pursues an honest course of open tryouts and the constant development of new talent is apt to enjoy a playing group of considerable size and variety.

One idea the community theatre director cannot afford is to choose plays for players, or to pre-cast. It is a constant temptation, but the final price in terms of narrowing the acting group is far too high. If the director can say to himself, "Judging by our past experience I believe we can cast this play," one more step is made toward decision.

At this point the stage facilities need mental checking against the demands of the new work. Again the university director, as a rule, has less concern than the average community theatre man. Educational theatre housing now encompasses many of the finest plants in the country and it continues to improve, while community theatre moves rather slowly toward acquiring adequate housing.

However, in most situations it is the talent available, rather than the stage and equipment itself, which first concerns us. I would rather have a fine designer and clever technicians on a stage which might be inadequate, than the finest plant with no one capable of using it. The off-Broadway playhouses, with all their modest technical facilities, have proved in Manhattan the production possibilities which have long been known to community theatre organizations in the rest of the country.

The Shreveport Little Theatre was built in 1927, and while it is a charming and workable plant, it is a far cry from many of the splendid new buildings we find from coast to coast. However, for more than twenty years Margaret's talent as a designer has given us great freedom in play selection so far as technical problems are concerned. Twice in recent years, however, she has proved my point in two productions away from the playhouse where she assumed the directing duties in addition to design.

When we did *The Women* in 1942, the many elaborate settings gave us a major production problem. It was with some surprise, then, that I learned in 1953 that Margaret was to do a production of the Claire Boothe play at the Officers Club at Barksdale Air Force Base. The stage was a semicircle with a twenty foot diameter. When I attended the opening performance, I was delighted to see that by clever use of such devices as reversible screens, the minimum use of furniture, and other space saving ideas, *The Women* had a satisfying design.

A year later she undertook a production of *The Medium* at the State Exhibit Building. Here the stage hardly deserved the name, since it was but a platform twelve feet deep with a curtain which, for some amazing reason, pulled across the last three feet of depth. Again the finished work brought an evening of complete satisfaction and considerable excitement with the emphasis on the music and the acting. Mr. Menotti would not have been displeased and would have been astounded to know that the entire scenic budget was under twenty dollars!

With decisions made as to the quality of the play, the probable understanding and enjoyment by the audience, and the likelihood of satisfactory casting and plausible solutions for production problems, the director can now regard the play as a definite project and begin the second stage of preparation.

He should now reread the manuscript and begin a determination of emotional objectives. What had made him laugh or cry in his first experience with the play? Was there a predominant emotion following the general story line? Could he begin to feel the flow of emotional values from one scene to the next? This period of study is to give the director emotional understanding of the work and is not unlike the period the symphony conductor spends analyzing and getting the "feel" of his score. It would be a backward orchestra indeed where this part of the conductor's work did not start until after the individual parts were passed out to his men at the first rehearsal.

This is also the time when the director begins to know the characters intimately. As he studies them, he tries always to find the qualities which make each different from all other people, written or real. Daily we see the marvel of infinite variety in human beings, and yet too many directors tend to group characters as types. If the human face with its few components can be so arranged that exact twins are a rarity, then surely the people created by a playwright who gives them backgrounds, emotions, purposes, minds, personalities, and stated physical details, deserve to be studied as individuals.

This is the antithesis of the old "stock" method of casting, the ludicrous result of which was an essential reason for the passing of winter stock companies from the American scene. It is an object lesson in aesthetic malpractice which may be re-studied on the television's late movies. As the nightly films unroll, we see player after player who had a long career doing the same character over and over again. If Mr. X was a "heavy" in his first films in 1935 and made the proper impression, we can see him in pictures for the succeeding years doing repeat performances, although in different clothes and settings. Our drama majors in the universities today may not believe that there was a time in this century when an actress could have a career of perhaps twenty years in theatre doing a line of parts neatly classified as "second business."

There will be those who will say that this individualistic approach to characters in a play would imply that rarely does an actor fit more than one part in a season. This is true, and one more sound reason for using a large acting company. We have found after more than twenty years that we repeat no more than about thirty per cent of our actors and actresses in any one season of six productions. Of course we still have the factor of "acting," which was too often mistaken in the "good old days" for the ability of an actor to assume accurately the physical, emotional, and mental qualities of any male character of his approximate age and type.

A simple clinical study in support of the thesis of using many individuals for accurate castings can be made by perusal of the *Playbills* of Broadway. How rarely do we find the same names repeated in a single season, or from one season to the next; yet most of the Equity members would like to be constantly busy. It speaks well for the quality of direction and casting in the Times Square theatre.

The director would do well to keep this in mind as he approaches tryouts in the noncommercial theatre, rather than the common tendency to recall vividly the star personalities who first did the play. Katharine Cornell and Cyril Ritchard are *not* going to be available, so it is healthier to erase the impression of the star personalities from the casting attitude.

This also helps to avoid the human failing of trying to copy the Broadway production which has been seen or read about. In community and educational theatre it is the *play* which comes first always. This is a vital premise which, if followed with fidelity, will bring many valuable returns. Among them is the fact that a sincere noncommercial production with first attention to the play itself makes the end result a different, and at times a more satisfying, experience for its audience. This despite the great stars and all the money which were involved in the Broadway showing.

Those who work in the other arts seem less guilty of this tendency to "copy" fellow artists. True, painters often group themselves into "schools," and musicians in the popular field move from one "type" of music to the next, and yet they know that success comes quickest when their own style of performance is recognized and approved. Certainly a midwestern symphony would like to play as well as the Philharmonic, but they do not attempt to sound exactly like it.

This period of pre-tryout preparation can well be spread over three or four weeks. Often it can cover a longer time span which may lead to further maturing of the director's ideas and emotional reactions to the play.

Balance is the double objective to be sought. A fine enthusiasm for the play and a sound understanding of the emotional values needed should be coupled with an open mind as to the individual players who may be used. If this condition prevails, the director is ready to begin casting his play.

CHAPTER TWO

Casting and Reading Rehearsals

T HE selection of actors for specific roles is a primary but difficult step in all play production. On Broadway, directors and producers work at it for long periods with all the wealth of Equity talent to choose from. The casting director of Hollywood is a man of extraordinary ability and high position. He, also, has chiefly the problem of choice, as actors besiege him for opportunities. Like his Broadway colleague, he knows that casting may determine, to a great extent, the quality of the finished production.

For the director in the educational or community theatre, casting presents the same intricate difficulties, and a few more. The talent available never matches in number the eager applicants who walk the sidewalks of Times Square or Sunset and Vine. Of the amount of talent present in the noncommercial theatre, much is latent or only partially developed.

To further complicate the matter, it is at this one point in the long series of production phases that the director is most often subject to outside pressures. The outsider, who may never have stepped on a stage and who certainly could not give a definition of rhythm, often blandly presumes to tell a director how to cast the play. Not that he would bother to find actors for a crowd scene, but he knows exactly who should play the leading roles.

This is not too prevalent in the educational theatre, although instructors have been known to put in a good word for a favorite student. The community theatre man may get such advice every time he walks down the street. Part of this is due to the fact that good theatre always looks easy, and no step in play production appears simpler to the layman than picking out actors for parts.

Because this casual evaluation has found reflection in some groups concerned with play production, we want to give careful and logical consideration to the entire process. How does a director go about finding the most suitable actors to match the images which have evolved during his preparation of the play? First, he needs complete freedom of choice; decisions as to the instruments he will use must be entirely his. Unless we give the director this freedom and this right, we cannot presume to criticize the final result.

While it is a disappearing device, we feel concern for certain community groups which still use a casting committee. Investigation has shown that this is often a misnomer, referring in most cases to people who spread the news of tryouts and try to find players new to their organization. This is all well and good, but for those situations where a committee actually has a voice in casting decisions, the hour grows late. Such an affront to the entire directorial concept ought not to be countenanced further.

The director has to select his material, and while the beginner may not do it perfectly, he is likely six weeks later to have a better play if he is allowed to use the personalities which to him seem best suited for the emotional problems involved. There is a sound pattern of preparation for the volunteer director before he attempts his first major production. When this is followed, and the logical progression of techniques are understood and applied, there can be a reasonable expectation of success.

One exception to the ban on outside advice at casting time concerns character recommendations of new players. The moral responsibility of theatre is moving steadily upward. This is true in all branches. The added emphasis upon family and children which fills so much space in the public relations of Broadway and Hollywood stars is no accident. It is part of a program to make the public realize that most of the talented artists of theatre are sound family people and excellent citizens. It is not easy, for any deviation of a famous personality, in theatre or not, provides the kind of reading matter which reaches the depths of mass appeal in the scandal magazines. The educational theatre is working toward the day when no theatre degrees will be given to persons of questionable moral fiber.

The community theatre can do no less than keep pace with its brother areas of production. It is perhaps even more important here, since the best of today's community theatre is based on the value of the work as a civic asset. Strangers at try-outs need references and identification. Newcomers in a city can glibly list activities at reputable playhouses in other locations. The time required to send letters back and forth is well spent.

The director's right to cast his play extends to the personal desires of the players who read. Actors are notoriously bad at casting themselves. Unless they are also directors, they can hardly be expected to have, or maintain, the overall viewpoint which makes casting an involved process of fitting personalities and talents into an aesthetic picture more intricate than any cut by jigsaw.

The two most common faults of players who attempt self-casting are to want first, a part made popular by some star in the

Broadway showing, or second, a part that is long. It is a failing of many noncommercial actors to think that because a role has many lines it is, perforce, good. As we have said, the actor's chief desire at tryouts should be for an assignment which is right for *him*. Since only the director has the finished play looming, brightly or dimly, in his imagination, only he can begin to assemble the picture from the material available.

To avoid this tendency of actors to cast themselves, it is helpful if the scripts are not available for reading until the appointed tryout time. We have never known it to fail that when playbooks are given out for reading purposes before tryouts, the director then faces, at the official casting session, a number of people with predetermined ideas about who should play what.

It is unnecessary for actors to study the lines of a play before first reading. The director is not looking for finished characterizations at that point, but rather emotional and personality values which will come close to those which he has evolved from his preparation of the play.

Most noncommercial players need to understand that casting a play is not a matter of a few hours, or even a few days. We hold two weeks to be the absolute minimum between open tryouts and the first reading rehearsal. This is a rather rapid timetable, and for those who are not too experienced, a third week for casting would be well. This may seem slow to some, but a quarter-century of directing has taught me that it is time well spent.

Mechanics of the tryout session are simple. A large attendance should be encouraged and an invitation to players new to the group will need frequent restatement. The surest way to discourage attendance at tryouts is to pre-cast parts. When the players see that the meeting is an honest attempt to begin evaluating available talent in its relationship to the roles in the play, they begin to enjoy tryout attendance. It is true, and can well be pointed out, that tryout readings are sound experience, as it is good for actors to read lines at every opportunity.

To maintain flexibility, the director asks players to read more than once and in more than one part, for it is the brief moments of personality revelation, the hints of emotional rightness, which tell him when a reading actor may develop into a proper casting.

For the benefit of newcomers, it is explained that this initial meeting is but part of the tryout pattern, the next phase being appointments for individual readings. This will be followed by a group reading of tentative prospects. Not until that point, two weeks hence, will casting be complete.

At the first meeting it is well not to read more than the first act of the play. Better to read through this twice than to go into the second act. Exceptions may be necessary when important characters do not appear until later, but in such cases, the reading should jump to a scene which involves the new character. By holding to a limited part of the text, it is possible to hear various players read the same lines; this is important in evaluation.

The session ought not to be too long. At this beginning point, it is wise to generate as much excitement and sense of the dramatic as possible. By their presence, the competitors show they want to be part of the production and anything done to increase their enthusiasm is good psychology.

This is also the time to ask those interested in technical work to so indicate. We have found the open tryout system a continual source of crew members. We also ask that those who want understudy assignments make it known. The meeting concludes with the director announcing that he will call back the most suitable candidates for private readings.

The director now confirms decisions on the floor plans of the settings. The designer will want to get the scenery under way and the fundamental elements of entrances, wall lengths, elevations, stairways, and other major architectural items have to be decided. Occasionally we find a designer whose chief talent is painting water colors, not done to scale, giving principally his reaction in color to the play. This is all very well, for color and decoration will have a place in the production scheme, but they have little to do with the blocking pattern which is a major step in directing.

Perhaps we lack sympathy with the gay sketches to which some designers give so much emphasis, since we have often found that their finished settings bore little relationship to the painted pictures. Many directors would gladly trade some of this imagination-in-water-color for basic realities in floor plans before rehearsals begin. The color and texture of a wall-hanging does not have much bearing on the director's problems and objectives as he puts his cast into blocking rehearsals, but it is very important for him to know whether the setting is to be eight or eighteen feet deep and whether the stairway goes up to the right or the left. Decisions about floor plans are needed at this point so that he can begin to think in specific terms about the broad movement of the play.

This is quite different from a system in vogue many years ago when the early directors would sit with miniature figures on a floor plan and block out all the action before the actors ever met on stage. Such an uninspired approach brought a series of proper geometrical pictures, but often gave a coldly static quality to the end result.

At this point, the lines of movement need be no more definite than designated entrances and exits, the general pattern of a scene, and freedom for the imagination to work in the general style of the play.

In this week following the open tryouts, individual appointments move the casting process ahead. Now the director gets to know the new talent and recheck the impressions given by the readings of his established actors. With new players, a definite attempt to discover basic attitudes toward theatre is helpful. A director is not a mind reader, but as a student of human nature, which he should be, he can learn much from the quiet conversation before and after the actual line reading. If the director and his group take play production seriously and work hard at it, the newcomer needs to understand this and express his matching or disparate views.

It is an excellent opportunity to stress the obligation toward rehearsals and to get exact definition of any time conflicts. Players are more willing, usually, to remove rehearsal conflicts before they win parts than after.

If possible, the private readings should be conducted in an auditorium or large room. Such factors as projection of voice and personality are quickly defined as the director moves about listening to the applicant on stage. Perhaps because of the dominance of the microphone today, we seem to have many "drawing room actors." They sound very well reading about a table in a small room, but placed upon a stage, their talent often shrivels down to the meagerness of their projection.

At the interview's conclusion, no commitment is made except a possible decision to have the player present for the group reading which occurs one week after tryouts. If there is doubt, or if other actors are yet to be heard in the same role, it is more diplomatic to say that they will be called about the group reading if needed.

In addition to getting clearer impressions of the new people, the director has to reevaluate his regular actors who have tried out. Like all good teachers, he looks for growth and development of talent. It takes discernment and ability to know that because a player did a certain part in a certain way last season, he is likely to do well in a larger assignment. This line of thinking occurs during the week *after* open tryouts when the available material is being itemized. It is somewhat the same situation the baseball manager faces as a new season opens. He has worked hard to develop new talent and make ready the old. Then the day arrives when the squad has to be cut down to size. It is not a time of easy decisions, and mistakes can cost games later.

The second group reading is such a time. To this the director asks the most likely candidates, often more than one for a role. This is a long session, perhaps more than two hours, during which the larger casting impressions are clarified. The director may find his ideas changing as the reading goes on. Perhaps the young man who sounded so well at the open tryout, and again in the private reading, now seems unsuited for the role as the correct personalities are grouped around him. And it may be that the girl, who had been only a second choice, reveals a rightness for the daughter as she reads with other members of the tentative family.

There is much for the director to learn at this meeting, and not yet does he have to make final decisions. In some cases he may be completely satisfied, but for morale purposes, it is better to announce that those needed for the first reading rehearsal will be telephoned. It is well to repeat the rehearsal schedule, and under no circumstances should scripts be given players to keep.

In the ensuing week, before the first reading rehearsal, the final decisions are made. In some cases, this will mean more private interviews, or perhaps calling two players back to read together if their relationship in the play demands a number of matching points. The questions of family relationships, range of voice qualities, matters of physical size, and other exterior factors—most of them settled at group reading—can be completed with a few more interviews.

We advocate not issuing scripts until the first reading rehearsal, which should occur about two weeks after open tryouts. It helps to build competitive enthusiasm.

It may seem that the casting plan is designed to keep the director constantly in command. That is correct, for we feel the discipline of theatre demands that it be the director's decisions throughout casting, that it is he who awards the parts. It is the beginning of the director-actor relationship. Unfortunately there are many groups where the supply of talent is small and where, sometimes, players take advantage of the shortage to inflate their egos and make casting difficult.

This is an infringement on the directorial concept, and one which would quickly disappear if there were more actors than parts. To players guilty of such self-indulgence, may I say that the paltry satisfaction of "being hard to get," or being difficult when cast, is a miserly return for the damage which may be done against the production of a play. It is a sure indictment, in such cases, that here again is a personality which does not really like theatre but wants the attention which theatre can give. To the director who has to suffer with such, my condolences, and the suggestion that the surest way to happy casting is to find and develop a plentiful supply of players.

Up to the first reading rehearsal we have not read through the complete play in sequence. This has been done with definite purpose, since to this point, our objective has been to find the correct instruments. We want now, for the first time, to bring the story of the play to those who will act it. Our objective is a relaxed, free reading of the' entire play with the story line predominant. There should be no interruptions.

For the director, it is an opportunity to check emotional im-pressions against the experience he had when first he read the play silently as an audience of one in the theatre of his imagina-tion. Of course there will be great differences; they indicate the distance to be traveled during rehearsals. Yet, if the two weeks of casting have been well and profitably spent, there should be a satisfying foreshadowing of things to come, miniature emo-tional values which can be grown to proper size during the ensuing weeks.

Let the players enjoy the play to the fullest. They are now their own audience, receiving in a different way the experience the director had when he first met the play. Discourage com-ment and discussion at this point; that will come later.

When the parts are given to the actors, ask them to write names, addresses and phone numbers on the inside cover. Sides, of· course, are the most efficient form and more than justify the work of preparation. They concentrate the player upon his own score, and do not confuse him as does a playbook.

The second and third reading rehearsals are short—an hour to an hour and a half. They include several objectives: correc-tions of pronunciation, and suggestions about wrong phrasing and bad readings. The actors begin to get some understanding of the play and its meanings—not specific, detailed definitions but general, wide-range impressions. The astute director does not stop at this time for discussions of the dramatic values or the minutiae of characterization.

We have known a number of young directors to waste valua-ble time at this point by asking players to give their ideas of what their characters mean and what the play means! There is no reason to expect that actors and actresses, barely out of the casting period, will have any valid ideas about the meanings of the play or about the basic motivations and purposes of their respective characters. It would be a simple-minded symphony conductor who would ask the oboe player to discuss the philosophy of a new concerto through which the orchestra had read but once.

Opinions are not needed, and ought not to be expected, from the actors at this time. Any opinions, especially those of value, should be in the head of the director. It is he who has studied and worked on the manuscript in detail. The fruits of that study will come to the players in proper sequence. They are trying now to get a general impression of the play and a start on the understanding of the characters.

The final reading rehearsal may well be scheduled on Saturday or Sunday afternoon before full rehearsals begin on Monday night. By this time cues are written for each speech on the blank half-page of the side opposite the typed one.

A reasonably long session, this final reading rehearsal should allow time to go through the entire text. The primary goal is for an increase of understanding. Some of the readings may be quite sound at this point; there may be a general feeling of wanting to get up and start the movement of the play. This is as it should be, and a healthy motivation for the first night rehearsal.

At this time, we give the players diagrams of the settings. They copy these on the last blank page of their scripts, not in great detail but with floor plans and furniture so indicated that there is some knowledge of the areas in which the blocking will begin on Monday night. With a comment about the importance of promptness, the final reading rehearsal concludes and the director prepares to meet his cast for the first full rehearsal.

As closely as possible to the announced minute, the director meets the company on stage. We have found that a rehearsal call ten minutes before work begins has merit. In our case, the traditional call is seven-twenty, with rehearsal starting at seven-thirty. The opening remarks state that the standard rehearsal plan is in three parts. Each night at seven-thirty the company meets for a briefing. This includes many topics, chief among them discussions of steps in acting technique. All matter related to the work at hand is mentioned with the sequence of each night's work outlined.

Immediately after the briefing, active rehearsal begins and continues without interruption. The session concludes with a critique of work done and any announcements about the next rehearsal. Rehearsals which begin on time close on time. We have always stopped at ten thirty. It is obvious that any tardiness will disrupt this schedule and waste not the time of the late-comer alone but that time multiplied by the entire company.

Amateur players, especially in community theatre, appreciate exactness in rehearsal, and will usually make every effort to conform. It is the director who sets the example, and it is un-wise to be negligent about starting promptly. We have found a simple device useful: to say that three o'clock in the afternoon is report time. Any player or crew member who has found that, through illness or other emergency circumstance, he will have to miss rehearsal, is to call the director then. This gives a margin in which to set up an understudy for that night's session and stops the damage done when a player telephones at seven fifteen to say, "I've been sick in bed all day and can't be there tonight." With the four hour cushion, the director can protect the rehearsal and the damage is minimized.

Since nearly all volunteer players have full-time jobs during the day, an efficient timetable has high appeal and the discerning director will soon have his company ready for the night's briefing exactly at seven thirty.

The first night's talk includes fire prevention. Even in the most modern playhouses, fire has to be treated with respect and continued concern. It is intelligent to ask that ashtrays are always used and that they are gathered and placed in a fireproof container at the end of the evening. The location and use of all fire-fighting equipment is explained. These remarks will need repetition at other briefings, particularly when settings begin to grow on-stage and conditions become more crowded.

A first night discussion of "the quiet climate" will do wonders for the entire rehearsal period. The stage is a laboratory where an intricate pattern of work is aimed at bringing a play to life. Anything which delays or disturbs that work is apt to make the final result less than it might be. As the actors start their important responsibilities in the project, it is essential that they have the best possible working conditions. Certainly an element which costs no money, and yet is priceless, is the quiet rehearsal area. Nothing can do more to upset and worry players than off-stage noise, especially voices.

Most groups can provide a room away from the rehearsal where off-stage company members can converse without being heard. From the beginning, there needs to be mutual agreement that whispering and talking are forbidden off-stage and in the auditorium during rehearsal. This leads logically to the policy regarding visitors. If we grant that rehearsal is, in a sense, a laboratory with a difficult and demanding project, then we have to ban all visitors if that work is to be done as well as possible. For it is the visitor who is first to violate the quiet climate with whispering, or laughter at mistakes.

If the director asks this of his people then he can do his part. Of course we know that the yelling, blasphemous "director" went out with the hansom cab, but today's *regisseur* can help build this atmosphere of quiet efficiency by example.

We need to explain also that rehearsal time is so valuable that there can be no general "breaks." In the commercial theatre, where companies can be in rehearsal for six to eight hours a day, the "take ten" has merit, but the three-hours-a-night sessions of community theatre go all too quickly. The person most affected by the "no break" plan is the director himself. All other company members have time away from their duties during the evening; the director alone is indispensable.

A concept which needs but preliminary explanation at this point has now to be clear in the director's mind, since it concerns the work ahead. It is that the play is to be treated as an entity. Long ago I recall reading "directing plans" which said such things as "The first week is devoted to the first act and the second week devoted to the second act." This is closely related to one of the many faults of the pre-director era. In that long ago there was not only little rehearsal but there were "one scene" actors who perhaps in retaliation against the stars who gave only cues at the few "rehearsals"—refused to watch scenes they were not in. There are tales that such thespians could be in long runs and never know what the rest of the play was about.

A play has a wholeness, the unity implicit in any work of art. Failure to understand the entity leads inevitably to faulty work in the segments. The director, through his pre-rehearsal study and preparation, has established a firm grip on the meaning and values of the manuscript and he has now to impart them to his company. It is not unlike the approach of the painter who must first "fill his canvas" before he can essay detailed painting, or the writer who starts with an outline. If the players are to develop properly in relation to the play, it is vital that they become firmly grounded in the entire procedure.

A way to build this approach is to ask the cast and crew to watch the first five rehearsals from beginning to end. We have found it important for the production staff, or as many as are on duty in the first week, to sit at tables at either side of the director's desk and study the play and the relation of their duties to it. They can make notes of pertinent points and facts on their clip-boards. The stage managers, the property crew, the electricians, and the costumers will better fulfill their assignments if they know the entire play thoroughly.

There is a double value in having the full company's attention through early rehearsals. They begin to hear the music of the playwright. As the characters move about and the rough blocking is completed, the visual impact of the work begins. It is different from the aural impressions which came from the reading rehearsals. Now there are moving human beings behind the voices; there is the first faint stirring of life. Within a few nights around the simple rehearsal chairs and tables, there are palpable imaginative foreshadowings of the creativity to come.

This treatment of a play as an artistic entity puts heavy demands on the director. He has to work rapidly to cover a sufficient amount of text. He tells the company that he wants to be able to take the entire play through, with rough blocking and business, by the fifth rehearsal. It is a formidable challenge but the work rate which can be established will do much for the ultimate production.

Eliminating the inefficient, the careless, and the inexact, sound play production becomes a series of orderly steps, properly learned on a planned timetable. The final result will be a well produced play.

CHAPTER THREE

Blocking

Blocking is the process which determines the strongest visual element of the play. The flow of movement, based upon logical dramatic reasons, strongly influences the ultimate values. Settings, costumes, lighting, and make-up have importance as sensory values for the eyes of the audience, but they are momentary effects, subordinate to the physical movements of the actors. Even facial expressions are of minor value in theatre. For our colleagues of television and motion pictures, the variations in facial expression are a stronger weapon, for they have the instrument for enlargement. The best directors of television know this, and it explains the growing use of the tight closeup.

The factor of distance in the proscenium auditorium tends to minimize the power of the face. Spectators back of the first few rows receive their important visual experience from the broader factors of gesture and bodily movement.

The early directors at times pre-blocked their plays, deciding on every movement before rehearsals began. This may lead to restrictive conditions which hamper inspirational and imaginative direction. At its worst, pre-blocking gives a wooden, puppet-like quality to acting. However, a few exponents still find some merit in the system.

32

The noncommercial theatre today usually does plays which have had previous productions, often on Broadway, and the director works from playbooks or manuscripts which have noted the original blocking. A constant question, therefore, is how much of this blocking ought to be used and what will be its effect on the personality of the new production. There can be no hard and fast answer, since it has to vary according to the abilities of the director, and because the printed blocking notes range in value, as did the talent of the director whose work they record.

Certainly the qualified artist-director likes to work with a clean canvas; some deliberately take out all original blocking. Again, there are many plays printed which define only entrances and exits. This is the most exciting method for the experienced man or woman, but today many directors are beginners. For them, it is probably best to start with the blocking as indicated and work from that foundation for variations and additions. In the most carefully edited playbooks there are usually several examples of contradictory blocking. A character is told to rise and then, several lines further down, a rise is again indicated. This means only that as the stage manager noted blocking on the original manuscript, the director tried more than one way of doing things, and in the transition from typescript to printed book the discarded direction was not eliminated.

There are several sound reasons for keeping early blocking in a fluid state. First, the players are not ready to absorb detailed direction. As they begin to move about the stage in the first few rehearsals they are learning in many directions. It is enough that they are told to rise or sit; the exact *ways* in which they rise or sit will come later. At the beginning it is a waste of time to strive to refine movement. We use the term rough blocking, for in this early period our goal is to "rough in" the movement pattern of the play.

Decisions have already been made about floor plans, and if they were sound, the director begins to feel a "rightness" about the playing areas. The noncommercial theatre, again, usually does plays with previous productions, and most playbooks have, in the back, line drawings of the original floor plans. They are not often to scale, but they do indicate the layout which worked in the Broadway production. Playhouses with expert designers often make important changes in these, but for groups less well staffed, it is rather sound to stay fairly close to the original diagrams. If Jo Mielziner, Peter Larkin, Raymond Sovey, or the other top artists are listed as designers of the original production, it is well to grant full credit to their talent before changing the floor plans too radically.

The danger of change for change's sake was seen in a production several years ago in a community theatre of high standing. One of the two settings was so planned that it occupied only the left half of the stage. Since it was used more than fifty percent of the time, the distortion and sense of unbalance seriously damaged the total effect.

The really talented designers know that their first obligation is to reflect the playwright's basic demands as to structure and locale. If these are seriously violated, it may be impossible for the best of directors to bring the play to life accurately and in full value. Changing locations of structural elements merely to be clever is not good theatre practice.

Fidelity to the original plan does not, however, imply that there should be a slavish copying of the first design. The economic factor alone makes this uncommon. When we consider that a single setting on Broadway costs from twenty thousand dollars on up and that a community theatre setting is often done for less than a hundred dollars, we know that the means to such economy brings many changes from the original.

Perhaps the most common fault among the more modest non-commercial operations is to settle too often for the square or rectangular box set. This form is the most difficult in which to create interesting patterns of movement. When the variety of blocking is further reduced by putting the chief entrance in the center of the back wall, the director is faced with an almost impossible problem.

This, sad to say, is the form in which most high school settings reach the stage, a result of the fact that the "standard" setting purchased from a scenic company is so "designed." In many secondary schools, where money for scenery is hard to find, there are rules about not changing, or even painting, the scenery. Thus, the secondary school director is often expected to direct in a floor plan which would frighten Elia Kazan or Josh Logan. Many community theatres are also guilty of this self-imposed restriction on visual variety.

A simple device which at once brightens the directorial possibilities in a "standard" setting is to shorten one side wall and lengthen the other. The "tilting" of the room at once adds interest and multiplies the possibilities for evolving interesting movement within it.

Equally simple, and almost as helpful, is the use of levels. Platforms are expensive to construct; but if nothing more is done than to raise the level of an important door leading to the hall, or to require a step down from an outside terrace entrance into the room, it is a beginning toward variety.

Occasionally, a playwright calls for the balanced rectangular setting with the key entrance at back center, but if he is wise, he wants the resultant stilted movement pattern for definite reasons. Howard Lindsay and Russel Crouse asked for such a room for *Life with Father*. They knew that the limited paths of movement would enhance the style of the play; millions of play-goers have enjoyed the added touch which this design gave their splendid evening of theatre.

Straight lines become dangerous if too much used in the floor plan of a setting or in the lines of directed movement therein. Angles, curves, and elevations add structural and visual interest to the setting and similarly broken and curved lines of movement gain value as stimuli. Part of the appeal of modern design in home building comes from the split levels, the interesting conjunctions of curved lines and straight, and the general "difference" in environmental feeling from the older, square-roomed American home.

The director has to be aware of this important aesthetic satisfaction which people find in variations of design and then try to use it fully when decisions are made about the floor plan of the setting. Today it is actually true that many theatregoers live in rooms designed with more excitement than some of the settings they find at their playhouse.

Exteriors usually give a free hand to those seeking variety, and yet they occur so seldom in modern plays that they do little to solve the general problem. According to our playwrights, most people spend most of their time in rooms and it is rooms they specify for their settings.

This predominance of the box setting is partly responsible for the occasional revolt against the proscenium stage. There are those who declare that "getting out of the proscenium" will give theatre a new freedom. We have seen several suggested solutions: the platform stage, the space stage, the arena, and the combination of these. While there may be gains in "freedom" for certain plays, it does not follow that all productions gain. I do not feel that *The Happiest Millionaire,* for example, will be any better, and perhaps not as good, when it is one day done on a space stage with projected scenery. Somehow, it and most contemporary plays belong in conventional settings, and it behooves us, accepting the fact, to make those stage rooms as interesting, as varied, and as accurate in color and decoration as we can.

Evolving a floor plan which does properly serve the play and also allows the director opportunity for a wide pattern of interesting movement does not, in itself, clear all difficulties. The arrangement of furniture, if done improperly, can defeat the skillful design and impose severe restrictions on the director.

At the 1955 convention of the American Educational Theatre Association held at the Los Angeles Statler, I chaired a panel on this question. Three able directors did brief scenes showing how the wrong and right ways of furniture arrangement affected direction. Amazingly graphic with live actors and actual scenes, the point came through that poor furniture placement in a stage setting could result in everything from awkwardness to monotony.

Blocking entrances with furniture is a common fault, as is the practice of using pieces which are so large that players have to squeeze their way around stage. It is also possible to place the same furniture so that in the first case it is impossible to find reasonable and comfortable playing combinations and in the second the director finds a multiplicity of natural grouping arrangements for his actors.

It is helpful to try for arrangements which look as if people "lived there." This, of course, quickly runs into the fourth-wall convention of the proscenium stage and another factor favoring those who cry out against it. So long as our audience is looking from one direction, most of the furniture will have to be so placed that the occupants will not have their backs toward that side. Yet even with this severe limitation, it is possible to do better than the sofa at right, parallel with the curtain line, and the two chairs with table between at left, sitting exactly on the same plane.

This convention of the proscenium never fails to disturb interior decorators when they assist in furniture arrangement. It hurts them that the sofa cannot be turned to face the fireplace in the side wall or that pieces cannot be placed along the curtain line facing upstage.

It is in the subtle touches—the slight angles, the variation in planes—that we can get variety. First and foremost, we have to keep faith with the play. Certainly the placement of the small tables and chairs on levels for *Separate Tables* is not exactly as it would be in a real-life dining room; and yet the deviation from the realistic is not enough to destroy the final goal—the *illusion* of the locale. The setting for *The Diary of Anne Frank* is a good example of fidelity in floor plan and furniture arrangement to the demands of the playwright, and still the levels and groupings give infinite possibilities for exciting movement.

It is in this matter that the arena stage perhaps offers its strongest directorial appeal. Here the "setting" does have four sides and furniture can be placed against the fourth wall. Now the lines of movement can be exactly as they would be in a room, and the "unrealistic" form of the arena stage becomes much more realistic than the proscenium. But for this gain a great price has been paid. Now there is no focal point for direction; the audience presents three hundred and sixty degrees of demanding eyes. What is shown to half that circle has to be less well shown to the other half. The clumsy devices of showing properties by holding them just above one shoulder or of using scaled-down furniture are admissions of the difficulties.

Thus far no one has solved the chief aesthetic problem of

arena staging: the inclusion of the audience on the other side with the picture you are trying to watch on stage. Those faces, arms, and legs across the way intrude endlessly into the arena actors' sincerest attempt to maintain a center of attention. Could this distressing factor be one day removed, there is still the difficulty of the form itself—the presentation at the center of a circle.

I have also noticed a tendency in arena staging to place two or three pieces of furniture in the playing area which are never used in the business of the play. If the items are solely decorative, we realize that they belong, since the furniture serves as "setting"; but if they are chairs, desks, or other functional pieces then they have the same detracting influence as similar pieces have on the proscenium setting. The unused chair, hassock, or desk tends to disturb an audience. For them everything revealed as the curtain rises has meaning and an implication of use. It is well in furniture arrangement to consider the possibilities of using floor space for action before placing an unused and unnecessary piece of functional furniture thereon.

Critics of proscenium decry the "picture frame" condition and we agree that it does resemble, in viewing technique, the spectator regarding a framed painting hung on the wall. Yet I know of no better way to experience painting. Certainly we do not gain by removing the frame nor by placing it flat on the floor and walking around it. The traditional positions of graphic art and the viewer are still best.

At this point, the arenaphobes may say, "But we are presenting sculpture." Their inference is clear; the statue on the pedestal can be seen from four sides. But is it wrong to suggest that from the rear we do not get the same aesthetic experience from "The Winged Victory" or "Venus de Milo" as that which engulfs us when we view these masterpieces from the front?

For me the arena stage charges a terrific price in aesthetic compromise but it does offer two economic justifications. It is certainly the cheapest way to present plays and it allows groups without theatres a way to begin production.

A final note for the company before actual movement begins concerns the divisions of the playing area and the stage shorthand used to record their positions. A veteran cast will not need this, but with one or two beginners in the company it is well to review the subject. Stage directions are always given from the actor's point of view as he faces the audience. Thus stage left is to his left and stage right the reverse. Downstage is toward the curtain line and upstage toward the back wall.

For secondary schools where the experience may be new to most of the players, a simple story helps to set the stage sense of direction. In the Renaissance, when the elaborate stage buildings with forced perspectives were popular, it was the custom to build the floor of the stage so that it actually sloped upward from the front. There are still a few archaic city auditoriums built in this amazing fashion, and of late a few "existentionalist" directors, in their search for ways to break traditional rules, have been known to use the sloping stage. On such an uncomfortable footing, players did walk "upstage" and "downstage."

Applying these two lines of direction, it helps to divide the playing area into nine theoretical parts, three from left to right and three up and down. Players then can readily begin to see the specific areas meant by "up right," "right," "down right," "up center," "center," and so on.

Stage shorthand uses the first letters of the location to signify the direction. With the letter "X" used for "cross," the amount of writing is markedly reduced. "Cross up center" becomes X U C while "cross down left" is "X D L."

It is widely known that we have discarded the ancient rules

about stage positions and movements. "Never turn your back on the audience," "Stand with the upstage foot forward," "The speaker always crosses in front," "Always make your turn toward the audience"—these and other relics from the primer days of direction went out with the schools of "expression." Unless you are doing a stylized or period work, the soundest general precept is to move as you do in life. Unless we work in this way we may build a visual pattern as unreal as the Delsarte gestures.

Many of the important movements of a well-written play are inherent in the writing. Often the playwright notes specific crosses and pieces of business which the character *must* do. This framework of the essential gives a skeleton of movement on which the director gradually adds the flesh of detailed and refined action. In the second scene of *The Great Sebastians,* Rudi moves from the dressing room into the little parlor to answer a knock on the door at far right. He has just learned that Essie is planning to smuggle the valuable stamp out of Czechoslovakia in her compact. As he moves, he knows that Essie must hide the stamp before he opens the door. To make his point he has but four words of dialogue while he travels perhaps twenty-five feet. In the first week of rehearsal it was enough that Rudi understood the purpose of the cross and that he began to get the "feel" of the pattern. Later it was enriched by gesture, two stops, and facial expression until this "moment" of perhaps ten seconds went into performance containing suspense, excitement, and a big laugh.

Rough blocking needs constant pushing if it is to go with any speed. There is no time for discussion; the player who wants to know "Exactly what do I do here?" has to be reminded that the objective is establishing the pattern and that "exactness" will come later.

While stage movement is best when clearly motivated, in early rehearsals it may be necessary for variety to set a number of unmotivated actions. If they are visually right and add to the movement pattern, the director can often evolve a motivation later to "write under" the action. Suppose in a two character scene that the girl has been on right and the man left for too long. Visually it is tending toward monotony. On a reasonable line move one of them across stage to give a new picture and then find a logical piece of business to fit the cross: the compact on the mantel, the search for matches, adjusting a piece of furniture or an accessory.

Do not press too hard at first for the whole movement pattern. Suppose you have scenes which are static in the first blocking. They can find solution as the feel of the play, and the setting, begin to build.

Sitting down and getting up are strong visual stimuli and can be overused. An arena production of *Dangerous Corner* left an indelible mark when I viewed it, in disbelief, some years ago. With the "realistic" arrangement of furniture which arena enjoys, the problems of Mr. Priestley's play ought to have been less than for the proscenium director, for in this rather conversational piece the full cast is on stage almost constantly. However, my colleague of the arena decided that to give the play "excitement" it would be well to fill it with broad movement. From the first blackout to the last, I never saw an arena stage so busy. It seemed that every actor on nearly every line either got up, sat down, or crossed. Since there were about as many chairs as characters, at times it reminded me of a childhood game. The result of this kind of directorial nonsense was that the real excitement which grows with Priestley's story line became lost.

Paradoxically, it is the inexperienced director and the experienced player who need most to keep in mind the real objectives of blocking rehearsals. The director with but a few plays behind him is eager to prove his knowledge and tends to stop for detail work while the veteran player is equally eager to know exact positions. Both have to resist these natural urges and wait for the timetable. The reversal of this situation makes for easier going. The established director knows what he wants at this point and the beginning player is quite content to learn that he can successfully move from "U R C" to the table "L" and record it in his sides.

A technical factor we deliberately delay until the second or third rehearsal is the marking of the exact floor plan on the stage with chalk, using different colors for the different settings. This definition of wall lengths, door, window, and stair locations fits better into the learning pattern this way. In itself, the indicated "setting" automatically starts a subtle refining procedure. Now the crosses have to stay within the walls; the distance from window to desk becomes an established fact.

For years we have completed rough blocking in the first two night rehearsals. It requires rapid, concentrated work and may well be too fast for many groups. Certainly this fundamental operation can be accomplished in three rehearsals, which means that on the fourth night repetition can begin. Things ought to move more rapidly now, with stops only to change obviously bad situations or to insert a few broad additions. It is not the time to learn exactly how the teacart will be moved; indeed it is not time for the real teacart at all. It is only essential that the player is learning that on *this* line a teacart is moved from this location to that.

Our regular objective for the fifth night rehearsal, which ends the playhouse work week for the actors, is to get through the entire text for a look at the rough blocking pattern. Again this takes rapid work, but on a three and one-half week schedule of night rehearsals it means that the production is running on its timetable and that later, and more important, points of technique will not be neglected.

The second week of rehearsal includes work on refined blocking; this time of progression can be helped immeasurably if the intricate elements of the settings begin to appear in actual form. We know that many groups have to rehearse in one location and do the actual production in another. However, in many situations the rehearsals are conducted in a place where completed parts of the setting can be used. Stairs, platforms and unusual structural forms offer formidable hazards to players unless they have become familiar with them through use.

Perhaps it is possible to produce plays which call for specialized settings—like *Death of a Salesman* or *The Diary of Anne Frank*—without using them until the dress rehearsals, but the performance cannot be too satisfactory. Certainly commercial veterans are not asked to open on Broadway in such settings after using them but three or four times. Creative acting is a completely demanding process if it is well done, and players cannot give their best if they are still learning how to use and live in the settings.

The best way, and the system which we have always been fortunate enough to enjoy, is to have the settings grow around the players as they progress through rehearsals. At the start of the second week, our outlined settings are in position, although certain temporary units may be kept only until the new section is built and put into place. This early use of the settings is part of our plan for adding all technical elements to a production at definite points on the rehearsal schedule so they are all familiar before dress rehearsals begin.

In the case of multiple settings, this means that the full crew works for most of the rehearsals and that scene changes are mastered early, thus assuming their truly subordinate role in the completed play. The crew heads, who worked through the first week at their tables along the curtain line, now know the production thoroughly and are able to direct changes rapidly from their set and furniture charts.

While the single setting seems to offer fewer problems, it is equally important that it have sufficient rehearsal. The chief factor which in so many groups leads to delay in finishing settings is procrastination, an unstated philosophy that somehow it is part of theatre to leave painting and even construction until the last few rehearsals. Some individuals seem to find pleasure in the confusion and frenzy of delayed production work. That pleasure is quite wrong and not worth the damage to the progress of play and players which it causes.

In many community organizations the stage is also the workshop, the only place for building and painting. The production work can not be allowed to go on during rehearsal time; it is no better to destroy the quiet climate with hammers than it is with whispering. Time *can* be found to do these craft projects away from rehearsal, and if a choice has to be made, it is far better to have a less effective setting than a less effective play.

However, this fitting together of the technical and the acting sides of theatre can nearly always be managed if the director and the staff will realize its importance. With the desired solution of the setting gaining form nightly around the players, the director can in the second week proceed to refinement of blocking.

He begins now to work in detail and to insert more "hows" and "whys" into the visual pattern. Crosses without motivation are re-explored and perhaps changed in length or direction. It is time to begin to talk of *how* the character sits down or stands up, although we will not discuss individual mannerisms and business until we take up characterization. At this time such general precepts as the difference between the characters who live in the setting and those who come to it from outside, are considered by the company.

During this second week, beginning directors discover, often with some surprise, one of the many truths about rehearsal progression. The players can now absorb direction twice as fast as they could the first week. A piece of business which ten days ago would have taken five minutes to set can now be done in two. There is no mystery in this apparent acceleration of the actors' learning rate; it is the result of building on past learning.

Now the general pattern of movement is familiar; much of the memorization of lines is past; there is a sense of being at home in the setting, and the furniture is more than a passing acquaintance. If the players are on *their* timetable, they are ready to begin using many of the hand properties. At this point the property crew should have assembled rehearsal props, keeping always in mind that the substitutes which are often necessary for rehearsal purposes need to be close in form, size, and weight to the articles which will finally be used.

It is regrettable to see the damage which can be done by under-rehearsed properties, even in such expensive spots as elaborate television shows. Few players can handle an article in a play exactly right the first time they try. It is because the human being in real life and the actor on stage are quite different. A man may have eaten two thousand sandwiches during his lifetime, and he ought to know all the problems, but give the actor a sandwich to consume on stage and a whole list of un-lifelike problems arise. In life it does not matter whether we can understand what he says as he eats; he can repeat. Again, it is not disastrous if he delays his next sentence while he chews. It is not catastrophic if he chokes a bit and has to drink a glass of water. These hazards, and there are many more connected with a sandwich, are deadly on stage. Here lines of dialogue have to be said on cue, in certain ways and in exact positions. Only a novice would think that such an everyday matter as eating would not need plentiful rehearsal on stage.

So it is with all properties. If a pen is to be picked up from the desk and used, that pen needs rehearsal—or rather the player using it needs rehearsal. And it needs proper vigilance. Players need to handle and know properties until they are a part of the character. They ought always to check the on-stage properties they are to use before a scene begins. Such an attitude implies a heavy and never-ending responsibility for the property crew, but it exists.

I recall that well into the run of *The Great Sebastians* a pen gave us quite a scare. As Rudi, I had rehearsed the pen and the writing of the dispatch to the papers in Act III for probably twenty nights. We had played for over a week, and yet on this night I reached the desk—and no pen! It was unnerving even for a veteran of many years, but knowing our playhouse had no balcony and that the desk top therefore was invisible to the audience, I proceeded to pick up a cigarette from the convenient box and use it to write with. Not too good a substitute, but the audience believed it and it gave me, once again, respect for the plentiful rehearsal and constant checking of all properties.

As players begin to run scenes without scripts in the second week, the director has to repeatedly warn that responsibility for recording new business and movement rests with them, for it is from this point on that good direction joins inspiration with practicality. The finest directorial touches are given during the rehearsals *after* the primary stages of memorization and the learning of the basic movement patterns. It is now that the true director, feeling the first pulsations of life in his material, finds his own imagination stimulated to envision proper readings, exact positions, and countless additions to gesture and business.

To keep the necessary pace, there is not time, either for the director or the stage manager, to stop and record these additions. We often have assigned the assistant stage manager to this transcribing, but the better way, the method which builds responsibility in the individual player, is to insist that it be done by the person to whom the direction is given. This means that the sides, even when not carried in the scene, have to be handy off-stage so that the player can immediately record the additions. The actor's script thus becomes a constantly growing record of his own character and performance.

This continued use and dependence on the sides as a personal and vital record is new to many players. I recall that once a young lady at the fifth rehearsal came to the desk at ten-thirty and said, "Mr. Young, you may have my part back. I know it now." After a brief explanation of the system, and a demonstration of its efficiency during the next weeks, the young lady checked in her script at the end of the run with this comment: "I really hate to give it up; it's become part of me. I never before understood how to use a script."

An exception to the personal transcribing comes in our organization when I want to add a long series of items to a scene. In the interests of speed, we often ask crew members to stand by and write in the additions as the players are given the new direction.

The company will gain respect for the necessity of this process if they understand that inspirational direction is the director's finest creative contribution, the antithesis of the older method of deciding every movement, gesture, and reading before the first rehearsal. Other artists, like the symphony conductor, are readily granted the right and dignity of inspiration. In his case, the acceptance may be helped by the fact that at performance he is the most prominent and seems to be interpreting the music as it is played, although his real labors occurred during the rehearsals. It might be interesting if for one incredible evening the director of a play sat at the center of the curtain line and "directed" with gestures even one-tenth of the items he had put into the play.

The talented, modern director is often so subtle that average players do not realize the all-encompassing nature of his work. Since even the legend of the screaming, temperamental "director" is almost forgotten, the quiet, efficient methods of today require keen observation for accurate appraisal. A few years ago Margaret and I sat one day on one of the smaller sets for *The Heiress* on the Warner Brothers lot in Burbank. Director William Wyler wanted Sir Ralph Richardson to turn his head in a certain way in response to a line from Mrs. Montgomery, the sister, who was off camera. Ten, fifteen, twenty times the speech was given and Sir Ralph would turn in reaction. It was hot, but the large crew was very still as they watched one of the great modern actors try to meet the director's wishes. At last, after nearly forty minutes, Mr. Wyler said, "Ralph, that's it. We'll print it."

The director alone, seeing the completed image in his imagination, has the urge to bring his human and material elements to an actual reproduction of that image. Like any true artist, he knows that perfection cannot be reached but that it has to be the constant goal. As he molds and blends, adds and subtracts, he sees progress. A great stumbling block, and one which is found in many groups, is the failure of players to attack and complete the problem of memorization. Its bearing on the whole course of the production is vitally important and merits the serious consideration of actors and directors alike.

CHAPTER FOUR

Memorization

Our scientific geniuses have not devised a machine which speeds or simplifies the process involved in an actor learning his lines. Even the gadgets under the pillow which are claimed to "induce learning while we sleep" have not proved of value in play production. Memorization continues to be a physical and mental process involving about as much work as it did when Shakespeare handed new parts to his players at the Globe.

Unfortunately for theatre, exercise of the memory has become less and less fashionable, and in the mechanical entertainment media, almost unnecessary. Radio has always relied on the reading of material, sometimes giving those who have worked long in the medium a serious block when they begin to learn lines for a stage. Memorizing for motion picture acting is a minor phase of the work since the objective of two completed minutes of film in an eight hour workday cannot involve too many learned lines.

Television calls for more study, and yet much of the material goes straight to the performer from the teleprompter or from cue cards—also known by the more stringent title of "idiot cards." The television plays broadcast "live" do ask that lines be memorized, and unfortunately they often suffer from failure of players to complete this phase of their work. It may well have led some TV producers to sacrifice the excitement of "live" telecasts for the surer and more accurate method of filming.

But in theatre, the lines have to be learned. Acceptance of this basic fact is widespread, but in too many situations it has been given the wrong evaluation. There are many theatre groups where "learning the lines" is regarded as almost the final objective of the players. This serious error may stem from habit, an ineffective director, or sheer laziness.

The director, as rehearsals begin, has solved many problems, such as play selection, casting, and production plans. None of these have needed the actors' time or consideration. They have come to the rehearsal stage with assigned parts, and need to understand their duties in the long progression leading to opening night. If they are more than mere novices, they know or feel that acting is a highly demanding form of expression requiring talent, work, and sound teaching. Although talent may be present, its translation into completed characterizations and integral sections of the finished play cannot happen unless they proceed through the essential phases at the proper times.

It is unfortunate that the first of these, memorization, takes concentrated study and is largely devoid of the excitement which surrounds so many other elements of play production. Study in itself, for adult community theatre players, is usually a neglected process, and one which in retrospect brings memories scarred with unpleasantness. Our present attitude in America tends to make study a distasteful but necessary undertaking through school years—one which, in most occupations, can be ignored for the rest of life.

Practice during the school years has made memorization less of a problem for directors in educational theatre than for their fellows in community groups. Certainly most players at college level have the incentive to learn lines quickly because they have chosen drama as a field of study. If there is an M.A. thesis on the difference in learning time for collegiate and community players I would like to read it; if there has not been one, it might be well worth the time and research. The high school director often does not enjoy the self-imposed stimulus held by university players, and often being in the high school play is regarded by the student as merely one more activity which will be listed under his name in the year book. In most cases, the high school teacher will need the same aggressive attitude toward this primary step as the director in community dramatics.

For it is the failure to make clear the importance of rapid memorization which leads to the deadly situation wherein the higher points of technique are neglected because players stay too long in the memorizing stage. In the vocabulary of the actor, memorization is but the Alpha. Until it is accomplished, little more can be done. And unless the study is complete, leaving no concern about remembering, the ultimate high goal of creative acting is not likely to be reached.

We have all seen, and I do not like to record this truth, many plays of which the highest possible honest comment could only be, "Well, they *did* know their lines." Parrots, and other members of the animal kingdom, can at last be made to repeat words, but never can they be credited with creative performances.

Are there wrong ways of procedure and bad methods of study which can be blamed for this evil of slow learning? I think so, and they deserve the strong spotlight of examination.

The first of the detriments is the elemental one of the form in which the parts are prepared. We have spoken of sides and their values, but we need to convince all directors that the surest way to delay the learning of lines is to give actors copies of the full play text. It is certainly simpler to buy a playbook for each member of the cast, hand it out, and ask that lines be learned; yet the mechanical difficulty of separating the lines of a single role from the rest of the printed page is an immediate barrier to learning.

Regarding the full text tends at once to diffusion of interest, no matter how carefully the lines of the particular role may be circled or underlined. It also, at times, leads to the disconcerting development of ideas about other roles, and even the play itself. Anything which draws the concentration of the actor from his own assignment will lessen the time and energy which he should be giving to it.

Typing the separate parts on half-sheets with only the cue line preceding each speech focuses the actor's attention on his particular work. At times, sides can be rented from playbrokers and they are more than worth the rental, but when they are not available, any reasonably good typist can prepare them. It is important that cues be long enough, four or five words at least; business is typed in parentheses.

During the reading rehearsals, the players write out their cues on the blank page facing the typed lines. They also begin to get an overall familiarity from the repeated readings. As the blocking begins at night rehearsals, they are ready for formal study.

Properly, the actor now learns one side at a time, studying the page of lines and cues, then folding it out of sight and looking at the opposite page of written cues. He answers these down the page, checking the one or two not yet learned. A return to the line page to study the missed speeches, and back to the cue page, will soon establish the side in memory. Then on to the second page, and after it is learned, a review of both the first and second.

This unit system, involving three to six speeches depending

on their length, is highly efficient and has the added value of giving a sense of rapid achievement. When the actor finds that he can learn five or six sides in an hour, the entire problem of memorization then breaks down into a series of reasonable units. These can be fitted into the learning schedule set by the director and repeated frequently. We ask that the first half of the play be fully memorized by Monday of the second week of rehearsal and all lines by Friday of that week.

When these objectives are clearly understood, each actor can see, from the number of his sides, exactly how many need to be learned each day. It is well to caution those with short parts to keep right on the timetable for there is a temptation to regard learning seven to a dozen sides as so easy that it is postponed. The players with the longer roles sometimes come in ahead of the deadlines as they find that memory, like other processes of human behavior, tends to improve with exercise.

Do not count on every individual being able to learn lines. Once in a great while a novice may show up incapable of memorizing. I recall only two serious cases in twenty years, and in both I suspect fear may have thrown a block across the memory process. However, like being run over by a tractor, it does occasionally happen, and the learning deadlines offer certain protection. In 1941 we were doing *The Man Who Came to Dinner* with a player who had done smaller roles cast as Sheridan Whiteside. When we got into the second week of rehearsal and the man had not memorized many lines, I became concerned. He did make some progress and we went into the third week before I realized that something, probably the size of the role, had so frightened him that he could no longer memorize. As sometimes happens in community theatre, the director was the best candidate for the rush assignment. I had the privilege of learning ninety-five sides in three days, but found the splendid role worth all the work.

Ten seasons later, we were preparing *Ladies of the Jury,* a busy play with many problems. We were into the second week before I found that the foreman of the jury could not memorize. Quite logically lenient with his replacement, we neared the end of the third week before the horrific truth dawned—the second man was also unable to memorize! On the verge of dress rehearsals, the only solution was for the director to again step in, a privilege which has many discomforts.

Another type who tends to disrupt learning schedules is the one who says "I cannot memorize until I know *exactly* how it should be read." These cases often reveal a slight acquaintance with commercial theatre, perhaps a summer of stock. They have inherited a thread of the attitude of the nineteenth century theatre when it was considered bad form to rehearse at all. Solution for this situation is further explanation of the process of modern acting—first, understanding of words, phrases, and sentences; then memorization; *then* characterization and all the other elements of technique required for creative acting.

Memory work for the actor is a continuing experience in which the simple outline of the words is established and their delivery and emotional values acquired by repetition and refinement. It would be a strange symphony musician who would refuse to play and learn the notes of his part until he knew exactly what final interpretation the composition would have. A golfer who would not swing a club until he knew how to drive three hundred yards, or a pitcher who would not throw until he knew precisely how to achieve a slider would hardly develop into experts.

The human mechanism lends itself well to the learning and refining process of practice by repetition. Yet unlike the musician, the golfer, and the pitcher, the actor is his own instrument. To improve the mental processes, the physical manifestations, or the vocal projections, is a matter for long, serious, and considered practice.

Only when the lines of a role are so completely memorized that recollection is automatic, or almost so, can the actor move on to the higher steps of technique. The truth of this is quickly demonstrated by the destruction of character, even of scene, which occurs whenever a player reveals that he is searching for a line. Interesting that while some of our most expensive television comedians regard forgotten or fluffed lines as excruciatingly funny, the theatre audience does not agree. In living theatre, belief on *both* sides of the footlights is a precious thing and he who destroys it does serious damage.

If we have made the players understand the importance of memorization and the obligation to complete it on schedule, it is but just that we explain fully the learning process so that they may have full advantage of their study.

Actors learn in three ways. First is the learning process through the eyes. While the good actor learns by observing life, and visual experience is an important part of the life pattern, our present concern is visual learning for the player with sides in his hand. Sides are the most efficient device with which to study cues and lines visually. As he sits silently in a chair poring over the half-pages, there is often a real stimulus in the number of sides mastered in an hour.

After this experience, the actor who comes to rehearsal and finds that once-learned words will not come out needs to know that he may have neglected the second learning condition—the stimulus which comes through the ears.

The *sound* of the word has to be learned in conjunction with the *sight* of it, which means that regular periods of study need to be vocalized. Often players with full-time jobs do not have time to have the cues read to them at home as they answer with their lines. For these individuals, the director should find space away from the rehearsal area and cue readers. At this stage the actor does not care about the emotional value or the voice quality in the spoken cue line; he wants but the words and their sound.

When visual and aural learning proceed together, there ought to be a marked speedup in the rate of line learning. However, neglect of study in a third area will do annoying things to players as they come from the dressing room chairs where they have faithfully answered every cue spoken to them and begin to move through the action of rehearsal. Lines well established through the eyes and ears become elusive and, in many cases, seem "forgotten."

The studied words are not lost, but until the actor has given sufficient study time to the third phase, the kinetic, there will be line difficulty. It builds respect for the complexity of the actors' work when players understand that the mere difference in physical state—movement as opposed to immobility—is enough to block well-studied memory paths.

Here, regrettably, is the learning process most difficult to practice away from the stage itself. To set the pattern of kinetic action and memorize it with the lines, it is essential that the movements be as exact as possible. We ask actors needing this study to arrange chairs and tables in the foyer or the dressing rooms, and as they study, to move through their assigned business. When the value of this method is clearly understood, many players will take the suggestion of setting up a simulated furniture arrangement in a room at home.

A disconcerting type of actor, and he is not confined to the amateur, is the one who wants to devote regular rehearsal time to memorization. There may be a few cases where extremely tight personal schedules leave no study time away from the play-house but more often we have found this attitude due to sheer laziness. Rehearsal is an ideal place to learn through the eyes, the ears *and* the kinetic sense; the visual and oral impressions come from the actual members of the cast and the environment is exact, especially if performances and rehearsals occur on the same stage. However, unless an extra week can be added to the schedule to provide this luxurious method of memorization, it has to be ruled out.

It is well to inquire of each player during the casting period about ability to memorize rapidly and to make certain that it is clearly understood that the organization operates on memorization deadlines. Most players will cooperate when the plan and its importance are explained.

Impetus can be given to the entire memorization problem if the "end of prompting" deadline is mentioned during reading rehearsals. This is the date, in our system six days before opening, after which no prompts are given. This includes the remaining rehearsals and all performances. Later we will discuss the purposes and benefits in detail.

Equally effective is to stress the point that the real excitement of creative rehearsal, the period of the actor's rapid growth, cannot begin until memorization is past. The players reluctant to accept this precept are apt to be newcomers who have never worked in well-planned play production. Or they may even come from a group where there was a certain "stylishness" in holding on to sides until dress rehearsal.

We have met a good many of this ilk but one case history will suffice. Mr. B. had been a community theatre actor for fifteen years before I met him for the first time. We tried to impart the learning timetable to him without appreciable result. He did not learn his lines until one week before we opened. He was an excellent actor and fine person, and I cast him the next season, hoping for better results in teaching the importance of rapid memorization. The experience was repeated; he carried his script until one week before opening. Then a desperate study session somewhere alone, and at the next rehearsal he knew his part.

At last we talked things through and found the reason for this painful scheme, which was unfair to the play, his fellow players, and himself. It had come about because in his early acting days, about 1920, he had worked with some veterans of the old school who did not believe in rehearsal and showed their resentment by carrying scripts until one week before opening. For fifteen years Mr. B. had followed the plan, until that "learning day" became firmly fixed in his approach to acting.

Gradually he pushed his learning time ahead until, at last, he was on the timetable of the company. The production was *Our Town* and he did a splendid job as the stage manager. During the run, as he enjoyed critical and audience praise in profusion, he stopped one night after the performance. "Do you know," said Mr. B., "I now understand what you meant by insisting that lines be memorized early. Never before have I had time in rehearsal to do the things we accomplished in this production—all those points of technique. They can't be mastered when you're trying to think what the next line is. I guess I never really did a complete characterization before. I never got to it!"

How true, Mr. B., how true.

CHAPTER FIVE

Characterization

A sound approach to characterization includes the assumption that the director has selected the proper instruments, that he has cast the most suitable of the available material in each role. This is one of the greatest favors a director can do for an actor. If he is right for the part, emotionally and physically, the time of creative acting will tend to be an experience rich in fulfillment for the actor.

This is the point at which many directors have difficulty with players who, through ignorance of true theatre values, judge roles only by their length. There are many actors both amateur and professional, who will consider "nothing but leads." That Broadway producers and directors ignore this attitude in preference for accurate casting is evidenced by the rarity with which players' names appear twice in a season, or even twice in two seasons, in New York.

A happier and more constantly employed group are many of the fine character people who do not ask whether the role is long but only that they are right for it. That splendid actress Mercedes McCambridge explained it well. She said that, for her, theatre was what she liked to do most and that she would rather be right in a small part than wrong in a long one.

In the noncommercial theatre this problem cannot be solved by pay checks, and often stems from players feeling they have "earned" leading roles by service in short parts. They need to believe in the integrity of a director's casting and to understand that theatre offers no richer reward than to be the right instrument in the right place. Implementation of this idea is always possible if the director never forgets one of the great virtues of educational and community theatre: he is not bound to the star system. There is no obligation of subservience to one or more virtuoso talents; a disproportionate amount of directing time does not have to be given to a "name" which will sell tickets simply because it appears in an ad on the theatre page.

With this happy circumstance, the director can divide his time and talent in correct proportions. Each of his players deserves, and can have, the time needed to make his role as complete and fine as talent and direction will allow. Appreciation of the high importance of matching quality of actor to the demands of the role needs to be taught in many educational theatres, certainly in those which use the system of letting the leads go to senior students who have "earned" them by undergraduate years in shorter parts.

If the primary objective of the university production is to develop the *acting* of the students, this method is valid; but if the chief purpose is to produce the play as well as possible for the pleasure of the audience, the casting will have to follow the other rules. The college situation in itself tends to give the search for the right instrument added meaning. While the community theatre usually works with players having an age range so wide that castings are fitted to the proper years, the college director has to cast all ages from a narrow band of years, running most often from eighteen to twenty-two. This does not imply inaccurate casting, since it is the *quality* of the actor, not his age, which is the most pertinent factor. But it does make finding that quality vital. In community theatre, if a man of fifty-five is put into a role which calls for a man of that age and general type, he is already part way to the goal; at least he will be right visually. At the university, however, if a boy of nineteen is given the same part, and lacks the right *quality*, the end result can be dreadful, since make-up and costume can never be more than just that.

Casting character roles in educational theatre is not too formidable if the director maintains fidelity to quality. Most young players are character types. Nearly every season, our friends from Hollywood, the casting directors and talent scouts, come by the Playhouse. Their search is always the same, for "the typical young American boy or girl who can be developed for stardom." These are difficult to find, so rare that I disagree with the use of the adjective "typical," although we realize that there is a wonderful, handsome, healthy "quality" about our youth. It is the magnification of the camera closeup which makes it hard to find exteriors like Tab Hunter and Natalie Wood which will please on the wide-wide screen.

In community theatre it is quality which dominates the casting requirements of the astute director, and yet in many organizations there are enough players in all age groups so that he can confine his search to the proper segment. Occasionally we find a casting problem which ultimately resolves in selecting a younger player for an older part because his quality is so right that it justifies the age differential. When we did *Jenny Kissed Me,* we had several actors of the proper age for Father Moynihan but they could not touch the personality and emotional rightness of a young man who tried out. In the end we decided for the twenty-eight-year-old and let make-up add the years. The result was exciting and best for the play.

The commercial theatre often follows this course. Certainly no one can dispute Lee J. Cobb's correctness of quality for Willie Loman in *Death of a Salesman,* although he was but thirty-seven or -eight when he did the role. He was perhaps the only actor of that age right for the part, since he was followed by Thomas Mitchell and other actors nearer Willie's real character age.

In reverse, there are some acting talents which seem never to grow older. Mary Martin's Peter Pan was completely satisfying, and Shakespeare's young women are most often well played by actresses of mature years. I don't recall seeing a fourteen-year-old play Juliet with much success.

Seeking and recognizing the rightness of quality, the foundation upon which characterization is built, requires a sixth sense in the director. Certainly it verges on the instinctive. It explains why the qualified director needs to hear but a single speech, sometimes a sentence, read by a player to know that this is the quality he is seeking. Confirmation of the judgment has to be found during the casting process, and once affirmed, gives some security in regarding the characterization evolvement which lies ahead.

Nurturing the inner quality becomes the primary objective and explains why the experienced director does not hurry to add the visual. Occasionally we have watched young directors in their third or fourth rehearsal spending time and energy trying to establish the posture, the walk, the limp, the time rate of a character. Often, no doubt, it is done through fear; not understanding the primacy of quality, they feel that if the exterior can be quickly established, the characterization will somehow grow inwardly.

This does not happen. Characterization, like any development in the life pattern, begins within. We need but to stroll past a few of our fellow men to gain a quick lesson. That man's scowling, unhappy face was not there at first; it did not *cause* his selfish, suspicious attitude toward life. The attitude, the years of hating the things and people around him at last left their imprint on his face. Of the myriad real-life characters about us, we enjoy most those faces which have been created by happiness. The clear, unafraid eyes and the ready smile are the visual record of a good and useful life. In the warmth of our contemplation, we forget whether the face is part of a body which has lived for thirty or for sixty years.

The surface dressing of a characterization is easy to add *if* we choose the right quality and develop it from the inside. It is like the speed with which a director can add detailed direction to his play once the company is firmly past the memorization stage.

With each player, the director has had private discussion of the character. There should be understanding of background, family, education, and major emotional viewpoints. By the beginning of the second week of rehearsal the player ought to be ready for further exploration. Now he needs to know how the character thinks and feels. In some degree, the mind of the playwright sets the style of thought, and in the greatest plays, dominates the thought processes of the characters.

As has been said, "Shaw makes his serving maids think and act like ladies, while his ladies think and act like serving maids." This dominant pattern of a playwright is not always so apparent, although an actor in a Noel Coward work certainly will find it easier going if he can think in Coward's brittle fashion.

The depth and quality of emotion also works within overall limits set by the playwright. We may defy them but we might reach some amusing results. It would be ludicrous to do an Arthur Miller play with the characters thinking and feeling in the manner of George Kaufman. This, I think, has been one of the weaknesses of the "method" school of acting. The darkness of emotional values, the pedestrian rate of expression and reaction, and its other attributes fit into rather a limited number of plays. Used in the wrong dramatic climate, they seem to be only emotional wallowing.

Fidelity to the playwright's encompassing demands is a primary responsibility of the director, and should be a basic consideration in every step—casting, style of direction, and the planned visual effect of settings, costumes, and lights. If he has done his work well, the players will tend to work within the bounds and should adjust with limited discussion.

What they must begin to establish are the variations in a character which make it *different* from anyone else, written or real. It is in the variations that distinction can start its growth and lead to a performance which has individuality. It is diametrically opposed to the stock company casting and acting plan. There, the same actress played Sadie Thompson in *Rain* one week and the girl in *The Nervous Wreck* the next. She probably did not have the right quality for either, but a change of costumes and a variation in make-up had to suffice. There were lots of lines to learn; there was no time.

The motion pictures are often guilty of miscasting for a different, but aesthetically no sounder, reason. Tied to the star system, Hollywood today knows that many tickets are purchased to see certain personalities and they follow the rule to some absurd lengths. *The Solid Gold Cadillac* was based on the comedy situation of an old lady outwitting the four ugly corporation directors. However, the film studio transformed the character of Laura Partridge to fit Miss Judy Holliday, with little benefit to the bright comedy of Messrs. Teichmann and Kaufman.

Exploring these differences can lead the director's and the

player's imaginations to the beginnings of creative characterization. For example, in modern drama we often regard butlers as little more than one-sided personalities. Recently we had occasion to explore the possibilities of two butlers: William in *Reclining Figure* and Maitland of *The Chalk Garden*. The first was the lesser role, but as the actor began to understand William's dominant ambition to be a primitive painter, and his stoic tolerance of the real artists and dealers around him, the character began to fill out and take on three dimensions.

Enid Bagnold's Maitland is a far more exciting role, rich in character possibilities. His prison background, the reasons for his presence in Mrs. St. Maugham's great house, his understanding of little Laurel, and his growing admiration for Madrigal all combined to make him, finally, a real flesh-and-blood man, highly entertaining for the audiences.

In the second week, there should be moments of fast, illuminating remarks about the characters. These can stem from the actors' questions, which ought to be asked before and after rehearsal. The director gives explanations as the scenes begin to develop. Points which would have taken fifteen minutes to establish during reading rehearsals can now be stated in one. The "why" of a line or action is made clear, and retention of the reason by the actor gives his whole performance new stability.

In *The Desperate Hours,* Dan Hilliard's walk up the stairs in the final house scene had been, for the first seven or eight rehearsals, only a long movement pattern. The actor had motivation. He knew that up in the bedroom was his little son Ralphie and the armed killer, Glenn Griffin. He knew that he, and he alone, had to mount the stairs and somehow save the boy. These bare facts were not enough. It was not until the actor doing Hilliard, well past the memorization stage, had begun to live the emotional experience of the tortured father and husband, that the magnitude of the moment began to appear.

Toward the end of the second week the actor walked up the stairs again and again as we filled in the man's thoughts—his revulsion against the convicts, his utter determination to get Ralphie away from Glenn, his emotional transformation from solid citizen to potential killer. Now the continuous walk up the steps was broken into four units, each with its own time, change of body and arm positions, and acceleration of desperate purpose. At last it was right. The Dan Hilliard who now entered the bedroom was beginning to be a man, different in many ways from all other men, different even from all other Dan Hilliards because he was being made from a real man who was different from all others. It was not finished. The actor went on through two more weeks of hard work before the completed Dan Hilliard was ready for the audience, but it was from this point that the full characterization began to develop.

This repetition of key scenes, late in the second week, until they near full emotional value is important. It gives the players a viewpoint; they reach a plateau from which they can survey the yet unclimbed emotional peaks of their roles. They have climbed one; perhaps they have, for a fine brief moment, become the character. This possession of one section of the life of the new person gives an emotional pattern which can be used, in variation, in other scenes. We do not try to carry this extreme emotional drive through the rest of the rehearsal for this particular character. We turn to another role, and if the player is ready, try to create the short reality pattern for him or her.

From the actor who has learned this strenuous lesson, we ask that detailed recording of the experience go into his script. How did he do it: what did he feel and why did he feel it?

There has been a plethora of words printed on the question

of whether or not the actor should "feel" his part. Diderot, as long ago as 1870, maintained that the good actor had to remain insensible to the emotion he was portraying; through the years he has had his followers. Constan Coquelin and his faithful have held that the player "feels" the emotions during rehearsals but not in performance. Stanislavsky, in a third school of thought, holds that it should be felt in some degree through all performances.

Despite Monsieur Diderot, acting without any emotional content eliminates the basic reason for living theatre, the communion of emotional experience by players and audiences. There are some veteran professionals who may give performances without inner emotional values, but often we have felt that bleak aridity across the footlights. The groundlings may have laughed or cried, but they never forgot that they were sitting in a theatre watching a "performance."

We hold that theatre is a higher form of creative endeavor than the perfectly timed manipulations of the juggler, the ventriloquist, or the puppeteer; but the actor who uses only the exterior of a character can lay claim to being little more than these. While it is a la mode for some of the remaining television comics to go up in their lines whenever they do a skit, I think the resultant giggles and the disarming air of "You see, it's just make believe," is an insult even in this cousin of theatre's. For a performer to resort to apparent or real errors for laughs is about as truly humorous as a pair of blowzy pants or a custard pie in the face.

How *much* emotion the actor feels is a different, and far more respectable, aesthetic question. This tends to vary as widely as one man varies from another in his emotional structure, imagination, life experience, and mentality. There can be no hard and fast level of emotion so long as we deal with living players. If we were to try to measure emotional content in a minute section of physical reaction, such as pain, we might find a norm but never a uniform standard. Confining this to the simple prick of a pin would, doubtless, find ten men of the same age, education, and background reacting to ten different points on the dial.

If this be part of physical complexity and truth, how can we expect a *standard* of feeling from a group of actors reading a line so simple as, "My, it's hot!" Working in such an involved area of human reaction, how can a director know when the actor has achieved the proper degree of feeling?

This is one of the problems which makes sensitive, accurate direction one of the most difficult and valuable elements of theatre. Like casting, it requires a subtle, deep, almost instinctive response in the director to human beings and their emotions.

Certainly, in the noncommercial theatre the Stanislavsky theory is best. Some feeling is essential through part of the rehearsal period and all performances. After years of study and observation, I have come to believe that it happens most of the time in good performances. It is not a constant and exact experience with even the most diligent, since the human being changes, though often imperceptibly, from one day to the next. Anyone with experience in theatre knows that the same player from night to night will more or less reach his creative objective. Actors often express it themselves in such phrases as "Tonight I really felt it," or "I wasn't in it this time."

Part of the necessity for its presence in the amateur theatre may lie in the basic motivating reason for participation. Some professional actors frankly state that their real reason for practicing their profession is to make money, although the great majority count the privilege of the acting experience as even more valuable. But most volunteer players do it for the experience alone. There may be a few who choose to act because they want attention, publicity, or merely to "show off," but they are, happily, rare.

This is why the proper teaching of the steps of technique, and a sound understanding of theatre's basic reasons for existence through the centuries are vital responsibilities of the director. Unless he achieves these, his players will not achieve the privilege for which they work—creative acting.

Even with the best of teaching, there will be occasional players who are unable to create emotional values. We have to be content to have from them, at best, the appearance of a performance. The only solution is to replace them next time with more capable people.

There are also those who try too hard, and think they are acting when they are only reacting to the experience of being in a play. This sometimes comes with youth and inexperience. Here a firm hand can turn the concentration away from self and toward the role. These are the types who suffer "stage fright," which is simply failure of the actor to work on the right things in the right way.

Slightly different from this type are those who go too far and let the emotions swell into control. From instability or nervousness, a player will sometimes really go into uncontrollable tears or anger. At this point acting disappears and theatre becomes impossible. However, this sort of emotional explosion happens most often at rehearsal. I do not recall ever seeing a player lose complete control in performance.

To feel yet not feel too much is the objective. We admit it is not a simple one, but to the high glory of theatre, it does happen with great frequency. This alone is sufficient reason to follow the plan we have outlined: establishing ideal working

conditions, making certain that every technical phase comes un-
obtrusively into the production at the proper time, and taking
the players logically and carefully through each step of technique. It is not unlike the way Knute Rockne taught football.
In his system, if every man in every play did his assignment
perfectly, the result logically would be a touchdown. Even the
Notre Dame gridders were not perfect, but in Rock's day they
did execute their lesson in his way a remarkable number of
times.

The way to establishing emotional values is as varied as the
actors present and the roles they essay. Some are able to work
quite directly toward the desired feeling while others will need
the help of the long familiar "memory of emotion." Here
again we are indebted to Stanislavsky for pointing out that man
knows only the emotional experiences which he has lived and
that the actor can often recall these for use in creating a role.
The principle is simply to find, often by discussion between
director and player: a past *real* emotional experience of the type
needed for the scene. By recollection of the details and concentration upon the past moment, the actor tends to recreate the
emotion within himself. When this happens, he then applies
it to the lines of the play.

Boleslavsky carried the principle to the point where he said
that recalling an emotion of the *type* would give the actor the
essential material on which to build. His colorful example was
the player who by successfully recalling his feelings toward a
meddlesome mosquito found the raw stuff from which to build
the emotion of wanting to murder.

Through this period of searching for and establishing the
correct emotional values, director and actor work with two
guide-words in mind: truth and believability. As the characterization grows, it has to be true to the play—the mental

processes styled by the thought pattern of the playwright, and the emotional range limited by the possibilities of the character. These are not restrictive conditions. A role which has challenged many of our finest players for more than three centuries is Hamlet, played by everybody from Edwin Booth to Eva LeGalliene. We could venture that in the best of the countless performances, there was fidelity to the thought pattern of the playwright. Shakespeare almost demands it! And not often has Hamlet been played with emotional creation ranging outside the reasonable limits of the character; yet the end results, the various Hamlets, have been as varied as the personalities and abilities of the actors, and the few actresses, who have done them.

This is part of the wonder of the discipline of theatre. In some respects, it is more exacting than that of perhaps any other profession. It demands the presence of talent and expects the proper use and development thereof. Through a long series of intricate and interdependent actions and progressions it asks that a long list of rules be scrupulously obeyed, not by one individual artist but by an entire company. When all this has been done, the objective—the play—does not come to fulfillment until there is a marriage between it and that great unknown, the audience. Unless both parties to the marriage are pleased and find satisfaction, the very life which has at last found creation may be abruptly snuffed out.

Yet within this rigid and apparently over-restricted discipline there exists a creative freedom greater, perhaps, than that of any other art form. It has the width of imagination, the length of human experience, and the height of creative expression.

If it is less than this, if it is merely the employment of a learned technique which puts on a series of masks, then we had best turn the whole affair over to the puppets and the animated cartoons, for they can do it more accurately and efficiently. Such an approach has little more value than the grotesque antics of circus clowns. If nothing real exists beneath the costume and the painted face, the ancient and noble purpose of living theatre has been lost.

Yet only by learning and perfecting the technical steps can we hope to keep faith with the purpose. It is this double obligation which makes the practice of theatre so completely demanding and, when met, one of the most satisfying experiences for those capable of creative expression.

This is a large concept for inexperienced players to grasp and yet remarkable comprehension can come when the students are sincere and the teacher is expert. If the emotional pattern of the character is understood, and sections of it have begun to assume form by the end of the second week, then the company can look forward with considerable assurance that it will reach its goal.

It is Stanislavsky again who has given us the potent "if" to aid in creation of character. Despite the misguided performers who believe that he taught to "be" a vase or "be" a chair, the great artist-director really said that players should think "If I were Peer Gynt, how would I feel, think, and act?"

As with most learning processes, the ability to create, retain, and reproduce the correct inner emotional values tends to improve with practice. As the players go into the third week, there should be a solidifying and extension of emotional creation. A few may have the entire emotional line pretty well in hand; all ought to be making progress. With this fundamental work well established, the company is now ready to dress the exterior. From this point on, all character props, such as canes, spectacles, wigs, and other appurtenances affecting appearance, posture, or movement should be used.

For now we are doing what we criticized in the directors who *began* building character with these surface items. Our players are using these things because they belong to the characters they have created from within. The reward is obvious. An item which would have been difficult to use when the play was being blocked is now mastered with alacrity.

It is also time to begin teaching the players any character make-ups which materially change their normal appearance. So often we have seen carefully prepared performances quite disturbed because not until dress rehearsal did character make-ups appear. Suddenly there were new faces, strangers, where the familiar had been. At a time when he should be concentrating on his own creative performance, the poor player had to become acquainted and learn to live with a new set of visual impressions.

As is often the case with technical factors, delay in inserting character make-ups at the proper time in the schedule comes from laziness or procrastination. We hold firmly to the belief that execution of his own make-up is part of the actor's technique and that competent make-up supervisors can teach nearly any make-up in a few hours.

Often it is well to suggest the "observation of life" principle at this time. If the actor rehearsing the doctor needs more surface material, ask him to observe the real-life doctors about him. Many professions, crafts, and occupations offer rich sources. Some experienced players have a valuable file in their own memories; they can recall many details because they learned long ago that the good actor looks carefully at life as he lives it.

When Ralph Bellamy was scoring such a success in *Detective Story*, we visited him backstage one night. He told us of the nights he had spent in the precinct station with the detectives and policemen, observing their life and the way they lived it.

Certainly Mr. Bellamy's performance was complete to the last exterior detail, and more important, it held truth and fire because Lieutenant O'Brien was a three-dimensional man, created in emotional values and projected by expert technique. Though we had known Ralph for years, we had not before met the character. In two hours we came to know a tough, fiery, New York detective named O'Brien. We never saw him before and will not meet him again. But we shall never forget him.

Each of the actor's steps has to be well learned, but characterization is close to the heart of the matter. To project the emotional and visual impression of the playwright's dream, to reveal the entire life span of a human being in two brief hours —this is indeed enough to give pride to the name of theatre. But there is more. Boleslavsky said of acting, "It is the recreation of the human soul through art."

CHAPTER SIX

Listening and Projection

T HERE seems a definite correlation between the increasing
noise of the world and our growing habit of not listening. It
may well be a logical adjustment of nature that the human
mechanism should show its protest against being subjected to
the increasing roar of motors, the clang of machinery, and the
crash of jets breaking the sound barrier. Certainly city dwellers
have learned how to ride with the clatter of a commuter train or
subway, struggle through the formidable sound of heavy traffic,
walk past the machine-gun volleys of riveters working on the
rising skyscraper, and finally enter their offices without having
"heard" any of it.

Noise has long since spread to the countryside. If one gets
far enough from the highway so that it cannot be heard, the
limpid quiet of the lake is shattered by the drone of outboard
motors, or the secluded cottage is hemmed in by the clatter of
farm machinery. Our writers seem to find no place so peaceful
that they can be inspired to write odes to nightingales, no
churchyard with enough quiet to bring forth an elegy. We have
filled our America with noise, and in self-defense, perchance
unconscious protest, we try not to listen.

This diminution of our hearing sense, whether it be from

77

protest against the noise of modern living or exhaustion from each day's sea of sounds pounding at our ears, is of concern to the practice of theatre. It dulls both the effectiveness of the actors and the receptiveness of the audience. We perhaps do not realize that much of today's communication is artificially forced on American citizens by amplification. Added to radio and motion pictures has been television, until it is natural for the layman to assume that any kind of entertainment will be turned up loud enough so that he will *have* to listen to it. This is true in his occasional sorties to the night club. Today's singer of popular songs has been raised on amplification. Have you ever tried to hear one when the microphone failed?

Theatre is not the only enterprise affected by this modern failure to listen well. Education also suffers. Most of my colleagues in the field state that their occupational hazard is the inability or unwillingness of students to listen. Much of this inattention is unconscious, part of youth's heritage of our times. Some of it is due to ineffective presentation by the teachers, who in many cases fail to realize the general breakdown in listening ability. The instructor who drones along, ignoring all rules of good public speaking, should not wonder that much of his material fails to penetrate; the students out front have not grown up in a quiet world and have not developed the keen hearing which was one of the attributes of that eager scholar who once sat on the other end of the hollow log.

There are many stories, allegedly amusing, told of our failure to listen. Perhaps the classic is of the woman who went down the line at a chattering reception. To each introduction she said, "I want you to know that I've just killed my husband." In each case she received in answer "I'm so glad to know you."

For the actor, listening is a twofold problem. He has first to listen with high efficiency to every instruction concerning the play and his work therein; in this he is the student and listens to learn. Secondly, he has to learn to listen as the character and understand the profound importance of this technique upon the audience and its reception of the play. For the audience will listen as the characters listen, no better and sometimes less. If we can make our actors understand the imperfect nature of today's real-life listening and that this will not suffice in the theatre, they should be ready to give full attention to the double problem.

Fortunately, theatre audiences still want to listen. That is why they have taken the trouble to buy the tickets, get dressed for the evening, make the trip, endure the parking problem, and finally take their seats—which are not as comfortable as the chairs at home and may be in an auditorium neither as well ventilated nor as warm or as cool as they would like. But they have done it, and now they want to hear and see the play. The verbs are in proper order, since the words of the playwright are the heart of the matter.

They are a different class, not economically but aesthetically, from those who are so often called "our vast television audience." These television viewers are, after all, only people who happen to have a box in the corner of the living room. They pay attention when nothing more exciting or pertinent calls. Their presence has required nothing more than being at home; theirs is not a positive participation. As for their numbers, I hazard that when we try pay TV we'll find the audience figures revised sharply downward, and it will not be due entirely to the cost. There is something about a free audience which makes its enumerators scarcely hold the sky as limit. We once knew a flower show which estimated its free visitors at "more than fifty thousand." One year they charged a dime admission and the count was sixty-two hundred persons.

Theatre-goers are a special group. They have paid the price in time, money, and comfort to sit before the play. By these actions they have indicated even more prized attributes: they are willing to listen and they want to believe. Perhaps only in churches do people gather in such ready acquiescence. That many-eyed, many-eared theatre audience is really a wondrous creature, deserving of our very best.

How tragic, then, that when so many curtains go up the audience is almost immediately mistreated. More often than with the badly prepared play or the illy written manuscript, we see it start with the inattentive player who does not listen well. This is desecration, regrettable and unnecessary. Since our modern audiences take their places subject to all the impairments of aural ability which twentieth century civilization has forced upon them, they must see the characters listen.

We can not say that bad listening is confined to the amateur players. Some of the most flagrant cases on record are those of tired road companies when the oft-repeated lines and careless management result in performances with no more attempt to listen, and hence no more illusion of life, than we might have were the lines repeated by a well-rehearsed flock of mynah birds. At best, this failure to listen in character results in a stage full of people who look like actors acting; at worst, it can be ruinous.

This emphasis on listening ought to begin with the first night rehearsal, when the director insists on careful attention to everything he says. Unless he can make his company listen effectively as individuals, they are not likely to learn and practice well the technique of listening in character. This is one of the reasons why, in the briefings and critiques, the director's voice is the only one to be heard. There will be exceptions, but the questions and the personal observations of the company belong either before or after the general sessions. It is hard enough to take a group of noncommercial theatre workers who spend their days in the clamorous, unhearing life of today, and teach them the importance of listening well. Every disturbance to this listening process will diffuse the attention and dull the lesson.

Realization of the full implication of this essential step gives added value to the *quiet climate* which we hold necessary to proper rehearsal. With this in force, the company has, at least, the environment in which to learn and practice effective listening.

From long experience, we know that the individuals and the companies which have listened best have tended to learn most, and in result, to give the best performances. At times this one factor can make beginners, or the players with lesser talent, able to learn so rapidly that they can go on to surpass the more experienced or talented.

In casting *The Bad Seed*, we were given the choice of ten possible Rhodas at tryouts. These were narrowed to four and from these we chose the principal and the understudy. Both little girls were excellent and won their opportunities because, with other factors equal, they were intent and accurate listeners. We felt they would learn quickly and well, essential for any child who was to play Rhoda. It was some days before we checked what we already knew to be true: they were both excellent students.

With the proper emphasis on this point for nearly two weeks, the company is ready for a briefing on the technique of listening in character. We need first to understand that proper listening leads to correct reaction, that requisite of all acting. Indeed, there are those who say that *reaction* is the basis of all acting.

Of our senses, we know that the dominant ones in living are sight and hearing, and that without them we tend to be locked in dark and lonely isolation. The actor who fails to use a constant stream of aural and visual stimuli to aid in motivation of his character's reactions is not apt to project much illusion of life across the footlights. The aural is the most important, for it is through sound that we give and receive the lines of the play. There is much pleasure to be gained by listening to a fine play without seeing—the modus operandi of all radio drama—but there is little for the viewer who cannot hear.

To listen in character is to project the sensory experience. Whereas until now he has listened chiefly as himself, hearing cues and giving lines with increasing growth into characterization, the actor now has to learn to listen *as* the character. This again has the infinite variety of the individuals written by playwrights. The way Anne Frank listens is as different from the way Saint Joan listens as the two girls are different from each other. Fortunately, the filling out of the character tends to make the listening process develop in the right direction. In fact, the two complement each other: the fuller the development of characterization, the more the player listens *in* character; the more effectively he listens *as* the character, the more three-dimensional his performance becomes.

The director can give added respect for this entire process when he explains that correct and accurate listening helps to build scenes. Whereas the scene played by actors who do not listen is a disjointed thing, the balance moving jarringly from one speaker to the other, listening players provide a solid base which is both emotionally and aesthetically pleasing.

There is a fine legend, though it may well be fact, of one of our great actresses who was going through the ordeal of rewriting in the preparation of a play for Broadway. The most troublesome scene was short, some seven minutes, with only the actress and the leading man. Try as he would, the playwright could not arrange the dialogue to achieve the desired emotional result. One day the actress said "Try giving him all the lines, and let me listen." Rather skeptically, the playwright rewrote the scene giving the man one continuous speech. Next day it was tried at rehearsal. By the accuracy and intensity of her listening, the actress built the scene so that it was exactly what was wanted.

When the company has learned to listen efficiently as individuals, and is making progress listening in character, it is time for the highest refinement of the entire process—one missing from many productions—the technique which does so much to establish that valued quality, the "illusion of the first time." Unless the actor in performance seems to hear the other lines for the first time, it is unlikely that he can project belief that the experience of the play has not happened before. Take away from the audience *their* belief that the events on the stage are as new as today and you leave them little—merely a chance to observe a repetition of learned lines and movement.

For this illusion of the first time is vitally interlaced with the whole purpose and reason for living theatre. It is this quality which makes it possible for players and audiences to believe together, and together to live the emotional values of the performance. This partly explains the failure of the motion picture to exert emotional dominance over its audience. There is a sense of redoing, due partially to the mechanics of the medium which insert themselves between the audience's emotional involvement and the film. No matter how deep or vast the emotions pictured on the screen, the emotional experience of the viewer is a personal one, quite detached from both the screen and the other members of the audience.

Once learned, the illusion of the first time is not difficult for the amateur actor to retain during a run which seldom exceeds two weeks. It is in the long-run professional companies that we often find this quality missing, to the detriment of the play. It is one of the reasons that the finest commercial managements insist on periodic rehearsals of long-run productions.

To effectively project this illusion of the first time, the actor has to be in full command of his characterization and to keep constantly and accurately in mind the sequence of purposes and the motivating reasons for the chain of dramatic actions. Thus, when clearly understood, it is an element of performance which ought to grow in value as opening night nears. As it does, the characterization grows in depth and sincerity. The actor cannot listen intently in character, permitting no interruption to the process, without adding to the stature and reality of his created person.

Our work until now—blocking, memorization, characterization, and listening—may all be in steady progression. Yet this pleasant state may have one fault which needs detection before we leave the second week of rehearsal. Our work, while sound, may be so intimate in nature that it does not carry into the auditorium. It is time we took stock of projection.

The first time the director leaves his desk and takes flashlight and clipboard to the rear of the auditorium, he may have some upsetting moments. What had seemed so encouraging, as he sat at his desk within six feet of the players, can diminish alarmingly as distance intervenes. A flashlight, or a clipboard with independent illumination, is mentioned to imply that the auditorium is dark. There are few factors, noise being one, more psychologically wrong for rehearsal procedure than a lighted auditorium. There can be little growth of illusion for the company as the bared teeth of empty seats stare at them balefully. I confess that it has always given me real physical pain to see a theatre with the curtain up and stage and auditorium both lighted. It is complete unbalance of the aesthetic pattern which reaches its climax whenever house lights are dimmed and a curtain rises. The lighted auditorium for rehearsal gives an embarrassingly naked air to the House of Thespis and makes impossible the air of theatricality which rehearsal so badly needs. Almost as bad are the cold and dim worklights which prevail on many rehearsal stages. For our rehearsals we have always used spotlights, with the gelatines in place, sufficient in number for illumination. It may cost a few dollars a month, but the gain in the way the actors look and feel in soft lighting more than compensates. It gives a subtle, helpful overtone to the total purpose: creativity in a place of illusion.

The lighting effects will not, obviously, solve the director's problem when he realizes that much of his play is inaudible or nearly so. His difficulties will not be so many if, from the first, he has encouraged his company to rehearse in full voice. There are two points which, made in the first week, will help raise the projection level. The players need to know that, first of all, they must be heard; they should understand that any straining by the audience to hear a particular actor will immediately set up an unconscious, but still real, prejudice against that player. They will begin to lose even audible speeches, and the performance can soon be seriously damaged.

The aural contact between actor and audience is not unlike that of radio broadcasting. As each character makes his first entrance he ought to know that there is a short period of "tuning in" required. The ears of his listeners have to become adjusted to this new wave length, his voice. If he fails to project at the level of the scene and makes it hard for the audience to hear, he has hurt his own work and, mayhap, the entire scene. Never forget that the audience can not "turn up the volume."

It is unfortunate that problems in projection most often afflict beginning players and are severest in large auditoriums. This double drawback exists for many directors of secondary school dramatics. Many high school students are making their first appearances on stage; asking that they do so in auditoriums of twelve hundred to twenty-five hundred seats makes the problem almost unsolvable. In desperation many high school directors turn to amplifying systems, a cure about as bad as the disease. I have yet to see a play using microphones and amplifiers with any success. In most high schools, there is either an attempt to stay close to four or five "mikes" placed about the stage, or if normal stage movement is used, only occasional lines are amplified. Under the first plan, it would be far better to broadcast the play over the local radio station and make it honest radio drama. Under the second, which has no value, the wise teacher will throw out the sound system and work for projection. Far better to limit the seating to the nearest four or five hundred seats and repeat the play—a gain for the cause of acting.

Beginning players, especially the young, cling with almost a moral tenacity to a determination that they will not "speak too loudly." One of our experiences gave an amusing and illuminating reason for this situation. In her first play, a young girl could not progress in response to my pleas for more projection. Night after night we worked, but still her lines carried barely to the front row. At last I came to her in desperation and said, "Why won't you speak up? Please tell me the real reason." With downcast eyes and a girlish blush, she said, "Mr. Young, I know I'm going to be just terrible in the play but I thought if I spoke very quietly, no one would notice."

Most often projection difficulties stem from psychological rather than physical difficulties. Once the player understands that the worst fault in theatre is failure to be heard and that

even inadequate performances may become passable if the playwright's lines are adequately projected, then the novice may
drop this evidence of shyness and fear.

Of course, many voices which come to the amateur stage
lack any formal training and may be naturally weak. While a
month of work can hardly replace a lifetime of neglect, certain
definite exercises may help materially. Nearly always, poor
projection stems from improper breathing and faulty breath
control. Early in the rehearsal schedule it is well to recommend
deep breathing exercises to the members of the company who
seem short on projection. Inhaling and exhaling to a regular
count, with conscious use of the diaphragm, for even five
minutes a day can increase the average volume of controlled air.

It is well to explain that using the voice at full strength in
rehearsal will give vitality to the entire speech mechanism. For
those needing extra work, the simple exercise of reading aloud
is helpful. The material can be anything, but a player's own
lines are probably best. A half hour a day in a room at home,
using plenty of breath and working for increasing volume, will
soon show results at rehearsal.

Even though the director does not move from his on-stage
desk out into the auditorium until about the middle of the second week, it helps to make a few short checks in the first week.
One minute in the rear of the auditorium will tell the director
whether the lines are at the proper level.

It is surprising that projection is no worse in today's theatre
when we consider some of the new difficulties which have been
added to the age-old ones of each actor's physical and mental
make-up. One of these is arena acting, which has more than one
difference from proscenium playing. During the recent re-
discovery of this form of presentation, a number of actors had
their first stage experience in the form. With the furthest

spectator no more than fifteen or twenty feet away, projection is not necessary as part of technique. In fact the drawing-room tone is all that is needed; hence many players have enjoyed success in arena although their vitality and voice strength would not be passable in a proscenium house. This is all very well, so long as the actors continue in the intimate form. Many have been the headaches of directors when arena actors tried to continue their style in a large theatre, for it is hard to convince them that projection beyond three rows of seats can be necessary.

The electronic tubes have to share the blame for some of the current attitudes toward projection. Players who spend time working over microphones—radio announcers, for example— have a difficult time readjusting to use of the voice without mechanical assistance. Perhaps of even wider significance is the general use of amplifying systems. Today the tiniest luncheon club cannot have a speaker without a microphone. Occasionally a public speaker with a well-developed voice will deliberately turn off the sound system, or move away from it, and the modern audience regards him as an oddity.

The commercial theatre has a real stake in this problem, for its actors do more acting over the microphones of Hollywood and television than they do on stage. Making the proper transition in projection levels is not easy, and at times the theatre suffers. Some years ago we saw one of our greatest contemporary actors in his return to the stage after seven years of motion picture work. We were in the fifth row of the orchestra and could hear but half the lines. That they were in blank verse, and that the longest speeches were his, did not add to the pleasure of the performance. However, by his next production he had relearned projection and his performances since then have been both a pleasure to hear as well as to watch.

There are definite twentieth-century connotations to the old problem of projection, and every director needs to be cognizant of them. Respect for the subject will grow in the cast if they clearly understand that there is much more to the matter than mere audibility. That is first; the lines must be heard. But then comes consideration of projection as the auditory evidence of the energy and emotional values which seize an audience and hold them. Why do we pay such fine attention when a Katharine Cornell, a Fredric March or a Ralph Bellamy speaks? Yes, we pay the obeisance due a star but it is more than that. With their voices they project an excitement and radiance which is quite apart from any visual impression. We can close our eyes but the impact is still there.

Though we tend to regard radio drama with almost historical interest, there are still exciting presentations in the medium. Here the entire projection of play, lines, character, and emotion is done with voice. Effective projection of this sort is definitely tied to conviction—the actor's conviction in, and of, his role. It relies on many qualities: sincerity, belief, a firm fidelity to Stanislavsky's "if."

So projection is much more than using enough energy and voice to be heard. It has nothing to do with shouting but is, rather, closely related to the general premise that a play is "larger than life." This enlargement is a quality perhaps unique to living theatre. Unless the facial expression, the gesture, *and* the voice are larger than life, they will not project to the patrons in the last rows who also bought tickets and deserve full value. This concept of enlargement leads to the final development of projection: the transition of casual and intimate scenes into the proper scale without distortion. We all know that good actors can "whisper" so that the balcony hears every syllable. The groundwork of proper breathing, voice training, conviction and belief which this implies is sometimes prodigious.

Yet it can be accomplished in a remarkably short time. A device to speed the process is to make certain that phrasings are not too long. We have seen many actors move on to proper projection when speeches were broken down into shorter units by adding breath pauses. Quite logically, asking less of the physical mechanism not only achieves the end result but often makes for more interesting readings. Carrying through a long sentence without a phrase mark gives even a veteran player a real problem in maintaining color and interest. By "breaking up" the speeches we are also using the dependable principle of multiplying the number of aural stimuli.

One of the few usable remnants of the "good old days" of theatre, that misty period before 1900, is the insistence which then prevailed that the last word or two or a speech had to be heard. Cursory examination of the sentence structure of most English and American writing shows that often the entire meaning depends on the penultimate words. Knowledge of this will make actors use proper breath pauses so that they do complete the sentence endings with proper energy.

Our two current lessons, listening and projection, are not only interrelated but of such importance that, once mastered, they will tend to bring forth performances of some satisfaction. Other and higher steps in technique may not be mastered; but actors who listen completely, accurately, and correctly, and who then project with the proper energy, conviction, and consistency are on their way. They are extending their creativity into the necessary zones; they are assuring their audiences of ease and intensity of listening. Their characterizations, while not yet full grown, are being projected into all the audience areas.

As listening and projection improve through the practice of

rehearsal there is assurance that the slowly growing creativity on stage will not be in vain. It should reach its target: the ears and eyes, the minds and hearts of that nearing audience. We have reason to expect that the intricate and sensitive process of living theatre will come to be. But there is more, much more, to be learned and mastered before the first night curtain rises; encompassing all we have come to know and all which lies ahead is one of the most valuable steps in the actor's technique: concentration.

CHAPTER SEVEN

Line Reading and Concentration

AMONG the common errors in the practice of directing is the tendency to expect exact line readings too early in the rehearsal period. How often have we seen novices in the profession waste precious time during the blocking and memorization phases trying to extract finished readings from their players. This is almost as distorted an approach to acting as the old-fashioned actor who refused to memorize until he had every speech "exactly right."

Only when the company has successfully passed through the stages of blocking and memorization, only when characterization has begun to develop, can we expect actors to approach accurate readings. For this is more than a surface process; it has little to do with glibness, possessed by some who are known as "good readers." Any disk jockey can do a fairly good job of "reading" the news, the sports, and the weather, but that is small guarantee that he can become a satisfactory actor.

True, during tryouts and the reading rehearsals, the director had to make casting decisions in part based on such surface reading, but we know that more important elements swayed his final judgments. The occasional flashes of emotional insight, the indication of values beneath the surface readings of the tryouts are the things for which the director watched. The happy castings are those in which the first foreshadowings of rightness of quality—seen almost in spite of, and not because of, early readings—develop steadily through the first two weeks and begin to give a solid, accurate foundation of emotional values from which line readings grow with increasing fidelity to character.

But at first we hope only for understanding. The meaning of every word, phrase, and sentence has to be learned. This refers to the simple dictionary terms, not to meaning in terms of emotional values, for despite our bountiful educational advantages, we are not a people of wide vocabulary. Sometimes players will rehearse words which are strange to them because they hesitate to acknowledge the questions in their minds. The director, by frequent and open use of the dictionary, and by stressing the point that words not clearly understood are not likely to be accurately read, can do much to make the seeking of exact definitions a relaxed part of early rehearsals.

Rarely is a cast assembled which does not also need supervision of pronunciation. This is quite apart from meaning and will vary as regional and colloquial differences appear. Fortunately the American theatre has now reached the dignity of position where it uses standard American speech in its native plays without that pathetic subterfuge of yesteryear, when it was the fashion to impose one or the other of the various English pronunciation patterns on all stage players. As a nation we may well be proud that our language is the most important in international usage so that as we do English plays on our stages we need only adopt a few key words and a widened pitch range to give all we need of British flavor. The Mayfair patois is rarely heard in American play production; its artificiality grates today.

One pronunciation error which still appears at times, even in a few motion pictures and television dramas, is the unreal effect of doing a play not originally written in English with super-imposed nationalistic accents. Only when the character—Italian, French, German or whatever—is trying to speak English or American, can we justify such mispronunciations. If we are producing *The Cherry Orchard* or *Right You Are* in its English *translation,* all of us, players and audience, want accurate use of that language. The use of accent does not give color, and there is no aesthetic propriety in it. The proponents of this silly chase for flavor would not disagree that there would be little gain if a company in Stockholm tried to improve their production of *Long Day's Journey Into Night* by speaking Swedish with an American accent!

Once the meanings and pronunciations are clear and accurate, it can be helpful if the players understand a few simple approaches to variety in reading. This is not a substitute for the emotionally correct readings which should develop as characterization rounds out, but is rather a basic approach to understanding the mechanics of speech and the possibilities of increasing the aural stimuli. It is especially helpful with beginning players who need every facility to engage in the art of acting with reasonable success.

Of the four general divisions of variety, the first is in *time.* Failure to recognize and use this element of variety is one of the most common faults of the public speaker. Maintenance of the same *rate* of speech leads straight to monotony and ineffectiveness. Most of us can recall a teacher or two whose ideas and material were good but almost impossible to grasp because the steady, monotonous rate of speech had almost an hypnotic effect. The clergy and politicians are not immune from this fault and it is almost frightening to think how the very course of human events might have been different if certain speakers had but learned to vary the time-rate of their deliveries.

A beginning can be made if the director will illustrate with a few speeches from the play the difference in effectiveness which comes when the monotony of a steady time-rate is changed to a varied pattern. A simple approach is to suggest that the more important words and phrases deserve *more* time, the less essential to be read at a faster rate. The overall time-rates of the scenes and the play are, of course, concerns of the director who needs also to guide the search for time variety by his players.

Not a substitute for emotional values, as we have said, this understanding and use of time variation will be helpful in developing correct readings as players probe deeper into meanings and sentence structure and come to appreciate that a succession of words rolling by at the same speed has no more dramatic interest than a string of freight cars rattling past. Working for this added color involves careful markings of scripts as new breath pauses are set. There is also a helpful correlation with work on projection as the shorter groups of words fit more securely with the physical energy at hand.

Variety of *volume* is not so often abused and yet its correct use is part of the players' preparation. A simple analogy as to the results of its disuse or use is to compare the steady volume of the average popular orchestra with the symphony's range from pianissimo to fortissimo. Graphs of the two sound tracks would show the first to be a straight, pulsating line with no variation to renew our interest, while the graph of the symphony would be a constantly changing line of peaks and valleys. The human being does still respond to the steady beat of the jungle drum, but the higher mental and emotional responses need intelligent and interesting stimuli.

In real life we do a good job in using variety of volume. In anger, excitement, joy and other strong emotions, we increase the amount, while with tenderness, sadness, and the quieter emotions we use less. If this tendency was transported complete to the stage, there might not be need for much concern; yet players sometimes fail to realize the full potential of this element of speech. We have already seen how hard we have to work to bring beginning talent up to the general projection level of the company. Within that range the director guides and refines the use of volume until it is correct for meaning and emotion. In theatre, the use of reduced volume can be as dramatically strong as an increase, and in some scenes, nothing is more powerful than a whisper.

We cannot forget that the use of this variety will not allow an individual actor to drop below the minimum level. While not quite so devastating on stage, the television player who refuses to bring up his volume to the minimum presents a formidable technical hazard. Skillful though the sound engineer may be, it is almost impossible to telecast a play successfully using more than one level in consecutive speeches. A few of our "method" players are guilty of this, and the desperate viewer has only one recourse if he is to hear the creeping vocalization of the one who is different: the dial has to be turned so high on the home set that all the other players seem to be yelling. The producers should know that many find it easier to turn to another channel.

The third of our varieties, *pitch,* needs attention because in our American speech it is commonly missing. Our narrow pitch range is, I think, a definite and logical result of our way of life. Although we are a splendid culmination of the blending of many racial streams, not one of them was potent enough to pass on the wider tone range of its native tongue. As American speech developed, with its basis in English and its countless assimilated words from other languages, we grew to speak it in our own special way. Much of this characteristic is. due, no doubt, to the sense of hurry which has long dominated our civilization. After a continent was conquered, the United States had to be built; an occupation which has never stopped.

This driving urgency, which has made us the greatest nation the world has known, has left little time for small graces. Certainly there has been no time to use the many-noted speech scale of the English, the Irish, the French, the Spanish, or the Italians. There *is* a difference in the time consumed in saying even such a brief phrase as "Good morning," between those languages which slide over five or six notes of the scale and the one- or, at most, two-note American way.

We are aware that public speech in that pattern tends toward dullness. One of the most damning criticisms of a speaker is to says, "He talks in a monotone." Though the criticism itself may be delivered on a single tone, the implication is clear; when speech is dignified by presentation from the podium, the screen, or the stage, we ask the pleasure of the color which comes from the wider note range. Of course one large segment of our film and television fare, the Western, has parlayed a set of ground rules for speech in an inflexible standard. A number of film actors have grown rich by saying "Yup" and "Nope" with even less pitch variation than their Indian opponents use with "How."

This will not do on the stage, save in an occasional gangster role, for we know that acting, being portraiture with emotion, needs to use every facility and all possible stimuli to project the created emotion. Our problem then, chiefly with novices, is to recognize their lifetime habit of talking with a minimum of pitch variation and then impressing them with the importance of learning to use a wider range. Listening to recordings of great players will soon illustrate the extent to which such artists use pitch variance. Appreciation of the voice as the audible part of the instrument (the actor) is sound motivation for improvement.

Use of a few simple exercises can often widen pitch variance. The first is to count from one to ten, starting on the lowest possible note and ascending to a high head tone. With some surprise, the player may find that it *is* possible to speak over a wide range of notes and, with practice, the range will tend to widen. Portions of the alphabet are also useful for this exercise, which should both ascend and descend the scale.

Application of variety of pitch to actual line reading is not as simple as our suggestions for time and volume. We cannot make any generalities about when lower or higher notes ought to be used. It is far more subtle and can be, like all four of our varieties, a helpful adjunct, but not a substitute for the correct readings which should now be growing from the inner processes of characterization and creativity. Yet the mere strengthening of previously unused notes and the knowledge gained from their use will usually become part of the improving readings. A tape recorder is of great value for the entire process of line reading, and preservation of recordings from first rehearsals for comparison with later work helps build the players' self-confidence and gives them a sense of progression.

Discussion of our last variety, *energy,* is the most complex, for it is definitely related to emotional values. Its absence from line reading gives a gray cast, a dullness, to characterization which is only to be desired when the role demands an emotional emptiness, a moronic flatness, or a similar quality. With normal and alert players who are mentally and physically strong, the flow of energy in line reading tends to vary in force as the lines and emotional situations move along the story path. Still there are players, sometimes with broad experience, who do not understand that they are failing to vary the energy of their readings. They will begin to sense its importance when we tell them quite honestly that full use of the varieties of time, volume and pitch are not enough; an unchanging flow of energy will result in performances which suffer from emotional, rather than aural, monotony.

This is a common fault with some professional comedians who work with exactly the same drive throughout their acts, and are unwilling to drop the level for their milder jests and raise it for the really funny gags. You can spot the points of error many times, for it is the fashion to insert such "asides" as "I should never have paid for that joke," or "wait till I see my writers." The less blatant comics, those who often give performances in a television situation series, seem to be longer lived with their public—and with their sponsors.

Variation of energy or emotion—we can almost interchange the words—comes from careful analysis of meanings and emotional values. It is part of characterization growth, and as such, needs attention late in our second week. It is not a surface process but rather a careful appraisal of the surface manifestation to make certain that it *does* project accurately the inner emotion. Since acting is communication of the highest order, any failure of the aural impulses to carry fully and accurately the meaning and emotion has the effect of static in a radio broadcast or poor transmission of a fine television program. The work done may be nearly perfect but unless it reaches the audience, we have wasted our efforts. For the actor is not fulfilled in loneliness—unlike other artists, he can not paint the picture in an attic, he can not write the book or chisel the statue in a room by himself—only the players *and* the audience can create theatre.

Proper use of variety makes intelligent use of the audience's mass human mechanism and its tendency to respond to a series of sensory changes and varied stimuli. The director works for these in rates of movement and adds the technical elements of scenery, costumes, lights, and make-up; but since spoken words are the life blood of the play as they carry meaning and emotional values from actor to auditor, it is imperative that they be sent with every possible attribute. I have always felt that Shakespeare's Advice to the Players was one of his sincerest passages, merely a rewriting, in more poetic language, of things he said often to the actors at the Globe.

As the third week begins, the director may find many readings and even entire scenes which are being read as he wants. It is wise to tell the players and ask them for exact reproductions at subsequent rehearsals, for variations in readings are nearing the point of no return. Three ways to record the correct readings are in the player's memory, in his script, and on tape. For while theatre includes in its ingredients many ephemeral things, among the underlined words of its discipline is *exactness*.

If we were to choose the one human attribute which most often made the difference between success and mediocrity—leaving out of our consideration talent and chance—many of us would select the ability to concentrate. This power to marshal all mental and physical energies and to command them to act in an exact and complete way can be one of man's most valuable possessions. We in theatre may come to appreciate it properly if we observe its potency in projects and endeavors far less intricate than play production.

In athletics it has come to be appreciated as the quality which makes the significant difference. The runner or jumper who can so concentrate that every ounce of strength is used exactly at the right time and in the right way will often win over a competitor who, having more natural talent for the event, allowed his concentration to wander at a crucial moment. It is almost the factor giving reason to the contest, for were it shared equally by all men, measurements of strength and muscle would indicate the logical winner, so why run the race?

Though the ability to concentrate may have some latent equality among reasonably matched age groups of Americans, execution of the ability has never been very uniform. Our millions of golfers illustrate the pattern. From the duffers who can not concentrate long enough to keep their heads down, to the near-champions who failed to concentrate properly for one disastrous stroke, it is most often the factor of difference.

In education our favorite whipping boy is concentration. How many thousand times a year do teachers say, "He isn't stupid. He could learn it, but he won't concentrate." Sweeping though this assumption may seem, it holds great truth. If we checked final college marks at graduation against the same students' entrance and aptitude tests four years earlier, we would probably find that differences in the comparative standings stemmed chiefly from the willingness to concentrate. For this taking command of our own resources—and this the actor must always remember—is not an unwilled process. We do not *happen* to concentrate; we have to *make* ourselves do it.

Like other human capabilities, this is also subject to the infinite variations prevailing among individuals. Regrettably, most of the American people have never given full and fair exploration to the possibility of developing this willed action. Furthermore, we are subject to a mounting popular philosophy, largely economic, of thinking it quite right to do less work so long as we get more money for it. We have almost forgotten the intimate kinship between happiness and the wonder of work.

Those who practice concentration, thereby doing their jobs well and finding the inner reward of satisfactory accomplishment, have, in some pursuits, become so rare as to warrant our delighted recognition. Today a waiter who concentrates on being the best possible waiter adds definite pleasure to a meal and wins for himself a public as loyal as an actor could wish. This is true for any craft or any profession.

For the practice and perfection of concentration brings a double return: it makes for good work, and by continually exploring and using all of the individual's powers, tends to develop those powers to new levels of performance. There seems a real similarity between the pitcher who achieves a no-hit game and the actor whose performance is described as "inspired." By concentration both have developed their inherent talents to where they can give performances above their apparently logical limits.

By sincere practice and conscientious effort, concentration *can* be developed. For some of the players who come to our stages this may be news. Through twelve or sixteen years of school, perhaps additional years at a job, they have heard the word and have been asked to try it many times. Yet it is quite possible for a man or woman to go through a long life and never consciously work at concentration. Unless those lives were marvelously sheltered or terrifically dull, the *process* of concentration has occurred many times. Moments of danger, distress, grief, anger, and all other emotional periods of highest content find the human mechanism concentrating with high degrees of efficiency. Because the average citizen does not recognize that this ability can also be applied consciously, he goes through the years using it unknowingly as a sort of emotional accelerator.

We have found it best in theatre to direct a company into the *practice* of concentrating before we take it up as a formal briefing subject. The absolute attention we have demanded for the director's talks; the use of sides which pinpoint the actor's own work; the "quiet climate" of rehearsal; no visitors; fidelity to the rehearsal timetable; all these and many more of our rehearsal procedures have demanded concentration by implication. Likewise the memorization period called for sound application of the principle, as does our continuing work on characterization, line reading, and listening.

Under ideal conditions, which do not often exist, our company ought to be displaying the benefits of effective concentration. While there may be a few laggards, the work record will indicate reasonable use of the willed ability. It is now time to discuss the subject and to prove the necessity for *conscious* application from this point on. Of all artists, none needs a high degree of concentration during performance more than the actor. The painter who lets his mind wander can repaint the mistaken brush stroke, the writer can put a fresh page in the typewriter, the musician will tend to play the notes correctly as his eyes follow the score, but the actor who fails to keep continuous and complete command may well injure not only his own performance but even the play.

As the importance of conscious practice of concentration is explained, a useful device is to illustrate the difference between its quality during the second week of rehearsal and the standard necessary by dress rehearsal. At the first point in most rehearsal schedules, scenes are gaining value rapidly, yet a slight error— a misused name, a twisted line—will often bring a general amused reaction. Destruction of a scene by so simple an outside force shows that the depth of concentration is still far too shallow.

Our objective is concentration so complete, so all-pervading, that the created play can live safely and undisturbed within it. Being a common goal, it carries mutual responsibility. This does not stop with the players but includes everyone back of the curtain line. Mention can well be made of the disastrous results which would ensue if one member of the property crew at one performance failed to place the necessary props on stage, or if the curtain man, or the electrician, at but one performance, was ten seconds late on a cue.

Since we are now going to work at deepening concentration, the actors need to understand that the process has to begin *before* entrances are made. Few of the oldest pros are successful at chattering in the wings and then, as their cue comes, walking on the set and into character. For most of us, a few minutes of concentration off-stage is essential for satisfactory entrances. This is not a passive, static time, for if we are to gain from it, our concentration is a positive action with definite objectives. We have long used a term for this moment of entrance preparation, calling it "getting into character." This has a general accuracy but it is not quite sufficient. Certainly we need to think sincerely, and recall accurately, all the myriad elements which have gone into the creation of our character. However, through repeated practice the transition of the actor into the role which began so slowly back when he was saying with Stanislavsky, "*If* I were . . ." now tends to happen rather quickly. The trappings which will come later—costume, make-up, completed settings—will help speed the assumption of character, although it will remain a measurable portion of time.

Yet there is another area for pre-entrance concentration and it is, I think, even more important because it guides and gives reason to the character. This is the *purpose* for which the entrance is made. Recollection, recognition, and crystallization of this motivating force before every entrance gives the actor a stimulus holding more than one value. There may be those who prefer the other approach but I do not think it is psychologically enough to say mentally before the entrance, "*If* I were Rudi Sebastian . . ." or, "I *am* Rudi Sebastian . . ." Rather, with the two or three minutes alone and the accoutrements recalling quickly all the facts of Rudi Sebastian, the actor should concentrate upon the positive line of action: "I am going into the room and through the French window to see if we can escape through the garden."

Now we have an entrance which superimposes on the character the drive of emotionally motivated action. The *reason* for the entrance is uppermost; by concentrating upon it the actor stands to gain doubly. First, he is not tempted toward diffusion of his attention which can happen when he thinks only of character and the many minutiae connected with it. Second, all reasonable factors should be in favor of his achieving his purpose in the scene, since it is uppermost in his mind.

When we did *Harvey* some years ago, I could not solve the problem of making the big rabbit come to life on our first entrance. I was too concerned with being Elwood P. Dowd and my concentration was limited to his various quirks and facets. Quite late in the rehearsal period I realized my mistake: I was not putting the *purpose* of the entrance first. Elwood ought not to be concerned with himself, but only in introducing his wonderful friend and desiring deeply that Harvey should be appreciated. That did it. From that night on and through the entire run, the audiences seemed very sincere in saying that Harvey was "real," that I had made him "appear."

When the character *and* the purpose are alive before the entrance, then our players are enjoying one of the many fruits of concentration. That it is essential for every moment of performance is, of course, obvious. As players begin to explore its values by conscious application, they nearly always discover that the return *is* double. The elements of technique thus far studied seem to improve at a new rate as better concentration speeds the learning process. There is more exactness in line reading and business, and even more exciting to the players, characterization and emotional values develop at increased rates. When the concentration of the company is of high order, the learned processes *and* creativity both tend to flower.

CHAPTER EIGHT

Timing and Rhythm

Our national enthusiasm for one, and then another, type of popular music through the years has led to such misuse of the words "time" and "rhythm" that the ever-present man on the street is not apt to give very accurate definitions. One of the early forces leading to this confusion may have been Ethel Merman who sang so enthusiastically, "I've Got Rhythm" as to give the word a new importance. What Miss Merman really meant, although it would have played havoc with the lyrics, was, "I have an extraordinary sense of, and reaction to, a time-beat." The Gershwins, of course, wrote music for singing, not logic.

In theatre we need to use more care with our terms, and directors and players alike should have always clearly in mind the truth of these particular nouns. Timing is the series of pulsations present in each line and scene while rhythm is the overall time value of the entire play which, generally, differs from that of any other play. A simile from another occupation may strengthen the outlines of the picture.

Chicago's Midway Airport has a personal rhythm; for any who have struggled through the crowds from, say, the Delta Building all the way to United Airlines, with increasing panic

107

that the maze of humanity might keep them from catching the plane, it is almost a beating, physical force. Within that rhythm are myriad varieties of timing: the swaying of waitresses' arms as they clear a lunch counter; the excited scamper of children's feet on the way to their first flight; the assured military step of the pilot and copilot on their way to take out Flight 406. Midway has many more, but all of them fit into, and are part of, the rhythm of that airport. And it is individual, differing in some obvious, and many indiscernible, points, from the rhythms of Idlewild, Newark, Atlanta, New Orleans, Dallas, and Los Angeles International.

But we wanted a sharper example, so let's return to our friends at Midway, who have reached the United Airlines building and found that they have just time to get on the DC 7 before it leaves for San Francisco. Up the steps, seat belts, motors starting, the careful revving up, and down the runway, and in flight. The contrasts between the rhythms of Midway Airport and the DC 7 at 18,000 feet are almost too much for one day. After the scurry and frenzy of frantic humanity trying to go in many directions in spaces which are too small, the effortless floating of the great plane seems truly of another world. There is unreality when the captain's voice over the speaker says that the ground speed is three hundred sixty miles an hour, for speed in the sky loses the earthbound sense of hurry. Gradually we realize our new rhythm contains its own pattern of time and timing. The expert movements of the hostesses as they add to the comforts of the passengers are unhurried but definite. Far below, the scurry and noise of the towns and highways are lost in distance and the earth seems to relax its broad face in friendly assimilation with our new sense of being.

Once firmly understood by the company, our defined terms

can become work subjects. Of principal concern to the players is timing, for their contribution to rhythm is one of understanding participation rather than positive manipulation. Of primary importance to the actor is to find the dominant time-rate of his role. This is related to all the facts of the character and to the type and style of the play. An overly simplified example, but one which will illuminate the point, is to consider the comparative time-rates of Will Stockdale of *No Time For Sergeants* and Angier Duke of *The Happiest Millionaire*. Both are young men of about the same age and race. Both are roles in recent comedies and yet the difference in their time-rate is so definite that it will affect not only the reading of lines but also bodily movement, gesture, and character reaction. Unless these parts are played with adherence to this time value, they may well be distorted, out of key with intentions of the manuscript and dissonant elements in the created rhythm of the production.

Failure to understand this keystone of all timing occurs most often in secondary school productions, where it is badly needed. As we have noted, the older roles in high school plays are often totally unreal because they are nothing but surface elements of make-up, costumes, and unmotivated distortions of voice and movement. Would that all directors—for community and university theatres often face the problem—understood that it is the variance in time-rate which is the chief distinguishing difference between youth and age.

Many are the sound acting lessons available to us daily as important personages around the world come into our living rooms by voice and picture. As we listen and watch we can hear and see that it is not the *quality* of voice which marks the older man or woman—often the years bring added richness—but it is the timing of speech which tends to retard as age increases. On his eighty-second birthday Winston Churchill was no longer the stirring orator of his "on our beaches and in our streets" days, but the voice was still demanding, the diction characteristic, and the quality holding much of the old color. The timing of his words and phrases told the age; more than fourscore years had left their slowing mark. Timing concerns far more than the speech rate, for its accurate application is required for the visual as well as aural elements of acting. To add age in bodily movement it is not always required that the feet should shuffle or the shoulders sag. Many older people have excellent carriage and a precise walk, yet as we observe them carefully, we can see that the impetuous spring of youth is gone and that the deliberateness of maturity has replaced it. Narrowing our scrutiny to the mere matter of sitting, we quickly see that teenagers sprawl naturally; they are somehow more comfortable if both feet are never on the floor. It may be that this animal restlessness of youth *has* to result in the antic dances which change names and variations in the jumping, but which do continue through the generations.

In most community theatre production the problem of adding age is of less importance, since casting usually follows the proper age range. This does not mean, however, that the time-rate of each character is less important. It has to be found by the actor and the director working together and, once established, carefully followed as a guide line for line reading and movement. This is not restrictive, for within the upper and lower limits of each time-rate there is space for endless variety; but it does mark the points beyond which the actor can not go if he is to be faithful to his character and the play. Developing a logical and continually interesting variety pattern within the defined limits does ask for precise and exact work from the player, a condition which ought to be present at the beginning of the third week. There is also a considerable safeguard in the system: it is a strong barrier against overplaying, and that equally damaging fault, underplaying.

For the director, it is imperative that he now firmly set the timing of each scene. This is an exciting part of directorial procedure and requires considerable skill and background, for the various single instruments, the characters involved, have to be blended into the proper time-rate without destroying their individual patterns. It may be well to point out that this is a very real and important difference between the technique of a director and that of a symphony conductor. The latter leads his men through various time-rates, but except for rare passages, they all stay on the same beat pattern. Further, the conductor is there at the time of performance to make certain that there is no deviation from the rehearsed tempos. Not so the director. For purposes of characterization and meaning, he deliberately establishes a counterpoint of speech rates and movement time. To set this so steadfastly in rehearsal that it will remain on time in performance is not an easy task.

The key to correct timing of the scene-units into which a play can be broken down is sound analysis of, and fidelity to, the dominant emotional value. In a well-written play, the scenes are a series of contrasts which sharpen each other by the simple device of being different. The Greeks did not worry too much about relief from one dominant emotional value but most playwrights since have been careful to recognize that change of emotional pace meant more attentive and interested audiences. Shakespeare was adept at inserting his clowns at exactly the right point between two long scenes which were pretty heavy going. Thinking in terms of the scene-units will be most helpful in setting the series of time-rates.

This delicate work is quite impossible so long as there is still fumbling for lines or slowness in picking up cues. You may have shared our experience of attending plays where countless times you could feel the players thinking, "Ah, that's my cue. I'll take a deep breath, get in the correct position—then I'll say my line!"

Such conduct on stage is unforgivable and results often from failure of a director to realize that there can be little illusion of life if the speech manner is so un-lifelike. Slow cues reveal cruelly the learned processes of a play. They proclaim more loudly than words that here are not real human beings living through a series of true emotional experiences, but only actors acting.

Correction of this common fault is not difficult and begins by asking the company to listen to life around them. They will find that any two persons of normal health who are discussing any subject which really interests them will converse in a series of broken speeches. This is predominantly true of the fair sex, as your ears may already have told you. Real-life dialogue is not a succession of completed sentences with polite pauses before the next speaker begins.

It is possible to illustrate this point quickly and colorfully by having the director read ten or twelve lines of a two-way scene with one of the actors. The first time through, both readers observe a breath pause after hearing their cue and before beginning the next speech. The second time both begin to speak on the last *syllable* of the last word in the cue. This slight overlapping immediately gives a lifelike quality to the dialogue which begins to have the excitement of living speech. This is done without destroying the timing of the sentence or the time-rate of the character. After this demonstration ask the players to listen the next day to people as they really talk and then to apply the syllable overlap at the next rehearsal. It will take a rehearsal or two for the company to achieve ease in the practice but within three rehearsals the play ought to move definitely toward reality.

An important side dividend which comes from the elimination of slow cues is that the directed pauses now become significant and take on meaning. Often pauses are among the high moments of a performance, but so long as there are empty spaces between speeches—slow cues—it is difficult for an audience to tell one from the other. Pauses, like other short measurable factors in timing, are set by count. The original three may be changed to a four when characterization and emotional values are complete, for they are always the underlying reasons for the time patterns. However, once a pause or a piece of business is set for a final count, it has to be kept. An actor cannot pause three counts at one performance and six at the next merely because he "feels" like it or wants to experiment. Exact reproduction of established patterns is a sound law of the modern theatre.

Occasionally we find an uninformed or misguided director who tries to establish scene tempo by stamping his foot or waving his arms. Such gesticulations will have to be left to the conductor; they work in music but not in theatre. The time-rates of players and scenes are most effective when properly directed in a series of variables.

We have witnessed directors at work who were trying manfully to correct a scene or an act that was "too slow." If cues were being handled properly and if reasonable time patterns were set for the various characters, the fault usually came from lack of contrast. Our sense of speed, or slowness, depends on comparison; without it we are not adept at judging how fast we, or observed things, are moving. We need the ground going by, the stationary against the moving, slow compared to fast, to give us a sense of rate.

The director needs also to recall that even the existence of the comparison is not enough to keep this sense from dulling when there is long continuity of the experience. On the highway, after an hour at seventy, we lose most of the impression of speed although we are still passing cars, billboards, and trees. Only when we come to a town and slow to thirty miles an hour do we get a sensory reaction. Then we feel keenly that we are barely moving, although if we stop to recall, we know that on our own home streets thirty is reasonably fast.

A continued rate, whether rapid or slow, leads to a sense of monotony in performance, and wonders can be done by deliberately setting scenes in contrast. At once the overall sense of time will become more empathically pleasing; the essential principle of varied stimuli will be at work.

While the actors give careful attention to timing and time-rates of their roles and the scenes in which they appear, the director has the solitary preoccupation with rhythm. In the early stages of his preparation he should begin to feel this encompassing pulsation of the entire play. With manuscripts of marked contrast such as *The Caine Mutiny Court Martial* and *Time Out for Ginger,* it is not difficult to sense the marked rhythmic contrast although exact definition of either work will take further study.

While rhythm is basically influenced by the writing, it is diffused through all the factors and appendages of production. Certainly correct translation of a play's true rhythm from printed words to performance asks that the visual impact of design be in key. Sharp contrasts again give illustration to the point. It would be an insensitive imagination indeed which could not visualize from reading the manuscript the wide difference necessary in designing the proper scenery for *Medea* and *No Time for Sergeants.* With slight projection, we feel certain requirements which would evolve in the colors, the lighting, and the costumes for these two plays.

Our contemporary theatre includes many kinds of talent. We find amusement, and occasionally concern, with the Clever Ones who proclaim that they are going to contribute something new to the sum of theatre knowledge by dressing an old play up in a trick design. It may be in the setting and the costumes, or it might be a jabberwocky idea like having three actors divide the lines of a single character and, like sets of Andrews Sisters, follow each other about the stage speaking in turn the good lines, the evil lines and, mayhap, the funny lines.

None of these stunts seem to quite come off, save in the eyes of those well-known "few" who would probably clap their hands in delight if someone produced a play backwards, for it would thereby be "different" and "experimental."

I cannot feel that distortion of a play's basic rhythm by such oddities is any real contribution to theatre. If we need three actors playing one role, or a setting made of ramps and step-ladders, let us have them because the *manuscript* demands it and not for some concealed reason such as the attention which turns to the one who walks out of step.

This sort of practice is not new and has happened most frequently to the plays of William Shakespeare. Modern dress, trick scenery, fancy lighting—all these and more have been tried but have any proved as satisfying for audiences as productions faithful to the obvious rhythms of the manuscripts, embodying the traditional costumes and, preferably, produced in the fluid manner of the originals and on stages like the Globe? In the other arts we would scarcely sculpt a bathing suit on the Winged Victory nor perch Whistler's Mother on a motorcycle nor expect to play Beethoven's Fifth with a Rockbilly orchestra.

This has not stopped experimentation and adventurous probings, but the other arts have used new materials. So also do we in theatre, but we find that experimental playwriting can often leave its audience so bewildered that it stays away from the next performance "in large numbers." This is the point at which the experimenters then decide that the only way they can try their tricks is upon established works, but because distortion of any phase of a play's basic rhythm damages the end result, they are, sooner or later, hoist with their own pyrotechnics.

Not all directors recognize correctly the rhythm of a play; the ability grows with experience and increased sensitivity. We like to think of the rhythm of a play being related to its timing as the quality of a day is related to its length. While one does not predetermine the other, yet both are important to evaluation by experience. Unless both are satisfactory, there may be no residue of satisfaction or pleasure. Recognition of rhythm often comes when the director first reads the play as an audience of one. It may happen when he first sees the work in production or it may not occur until there has been some time spent on preparation, but it is an aesthetic recognition which the director has to experience if he is to bring a proper directorial concept to the play.

This recognition process is not necessarily uniform for all directors, yet the differences are related to details of personal reactions rather than acceptance or rejection of the rhythm as a whole.

I happened to see *The Cocktail Party* before I read it. While the excellent Broadway company gave me a splendid experience in theatre, I found, upon studying the manuscript, that I wanted to do our production with important differences in both timing and interpretation of rhythm. It seemed to me that some of the bewilderment and lack of understanding expressed by average men and women about the New York showing came not essentially from Eliot's writing but from a general time-rate which was too fast, particularly with the element of British speech which was used. The audiences were having a hard time understanding what was *said*, when they well needed their full time to understand what was *meant*. It also seemed to me that the play could be more human and not kept so clearly on the plane of intellectually cold discussion.

These ideas would probably not have met concurrence from the playwright but we had to do the play for *our* audiences and we wanted them to take away from *The Cocktail Party* as much as we could give them. Setting a generally slower time-rate and working for clarity of speech rather than excessive Britishness, we saw in late rehearsals that the play would be easy to hear and thereby, we hoped, easier to understand. These were changes in timing. I then worked to increase the humanity of the characters, to make them warmer and more three-dimensional. I liked them and I wanted the audience to like them, not just to listen to their discussions. While this was an adjustment of the rhythm as the play was produced on Broadway, it was keeping solid faith with my own conception of quality; and for our audiences, it was a wise decision. Our production came through clearly and with enlarged human values. While we would not compare our actors with the star-studded New York company, we think their performances may have given our audiences a deeper and clearer experience of Eliot's *play*. If it happened, our objective was achieved.

All discussions of rhythm in theatre are bound to consider the audience and to realize that it, too, possesses a rhythm which is variable. Unless there are points of contact between the rhythms of play and audience, there is a chance that not much real theatre occurs. This is what actors are talking about when they ask, after the first few scenes, "How's the audience?" Experienced players know how the same performance, repeated as exactly as the human factors permit, can be many different experiences, depending on the many-bodied creature out front.

So many times through the years we have seen dismayed playwrights and producers standing in the back of the theatre during and after a Broadway first night and have heard them sadly say, "It wasn't like this at the preview performances." The factor of difference, the rhythm of the Broadway first-nighters, has, I think, ruined plays which deserved a better fate. Certainly the late-comers, the preponderance of those who come to be seen rather than to see, and the general coldness and rudeness of that first-night audience is not conducive to success. A play needs great strength to superimpose its rhythm on this strange mixture of unfriendly qualities. We have, at times, been surprised to learn next day that we were present the night before at the premiere of a new hit. After the opening night of *Witness for the Prosecution* we discussed its chances. We felt it a very good mystery and well played but we agreed that the audience did not seem impressed. Fortunately, the first-nighters do not come back, and hundreds of other audiences have agreed that "Witness" is a hit. One day we may evolve a plan where there is no "first night" and critics will get their first experience of the play under normal conditions with normal audiences. That may mark a new era of man's humanity to theatre.

While "first nightness" is a special sort of blemish on theatre-going, there are other influences which change audience rhythm. These can range from national or world tensions through weather conditions. We happened to see the matinee performance of *The Lady's Not for Burning* on the day a hurricane-force storm struck New York. By the time we reached the theatre, Forty-Fourth Street was roped off because the huge sign of the Lincoln Hotel had been blown loose from all but one of its moorings and swung high in the air like some fantastic Diocletian sword. The police and firemen guided the play-goers past the barricades and we found ourselves snug in the theatre and anticipating the Fry play.

However, the wind roared all afternoon so loudly that John Gielgud, Vanessa Brown, and the others had to double their projection. Before the last scene, Mr. Gielgud came before the curtain and asked the audience to leave by the side exits since the dangers in front of the theatre were still there. The actors did nobly, but the audience could not find contact with the play. An extreme example of the weather factor; but we have seen it occur in lesser degrees from audiences who have struggled through rain or snow and who find a theatre too warm or too cold. The rhythm of an audience is far more fragile and infinitely more variable than that of the play they have come to see. Play-goers on different nights, who are in complete disagreement about a play, may well be speaking in complete honesty. Yet if the play is well done and the company competent, the fault for the performance which was unsatisfactory may be not with those upon the stage, but with those who bought the tickets.

This requisite matching of rhythms, of overall qualities, for satisfactory culmination of an artistic experience is not confined to theatre. It may be that in the other arts, audiences do a better job of finding their way to the proper auditorium. It is hard to imagine a more dismayed group than would be the country music audience which found itself at a Philharmonic concert, unless it would be the symphony audience which discovered that their tickets had seated them at a performance of the Grand Old Opry.

This is perhaps the underlying reason for the continued rise of the musical comedy form as the dominant Broadway production type. Their rhythm matches that of the transient ticket-holders who insist that their New York leisure time be devoted to having fun. Even the theatre parties which are herded in from the boroughs are in a holiday mood; they want music and laughter, not deep emotions and tragedy. Does this not help explain the almost amusing acceptance of plays, which otherwise have limited popular appeal, once they are translated to the musical form? We can hardly believe that a flawless production of *They Knew What They Wanted* would enjoy half the run which has been accorded *The Most Happy Fella,* nor that *Anna Christie* could have one-fourth the cordial reception given *New Girl in Town.*

Forecasts need time for confirmation, but if the trend continues, production on Broadway may one day be confined to the musical form with straight plays relegated to the smaller but perhaps truer theatre audiences of off-Broadway.

A guide for the director in crystallizing his decisions about the rhythm of the production is to understand the broad outlines of the general type into which it falls. This is not a complete process, for rhythmic interpretation is at best closely related to the entire creative concept of a director. A certain classification may help those who are early in their directorial careers.

Comedy projects a rhythm so positive that it would seem difficult not to recognize its general requirements. It is gay, bright, of light emotional values, and designed to amuse. Yet knowledge of these general demands does not prevent some producing groups from handicapping their project at the start by such childish errors as planning a setting so somber in color values that Bert Lahr could not be funny in it. We have seen other productions where settings were in key but ruined by a "mood" electrician who devised a lighting plan more suitable for *Bury the Dead.* Our point is that the director has to be vigilant to make certain that production elements do not veer away from the general rhythm to result in later serious damage. These are adjacent to, but have important bearing on, the development of correct rhythm through the rehearsal period.

It is possible to think in the comic vein through these steps and yet be wrong because the correct type of comedy was not kept in mind. Drawing room comedy has its own special set of demands which asks of all production elements that they be polite, well mannered, and sophisticated. A mistake like casting an oafish actor in the Basil Rathbone role in *Jane* can throw the rhythmic pattern so off balance as to ruin the entire play.

For domestic comedy we seek the middle ground: comfortable, easily recognizable, with a prevalence of a warm and friendly atmosphere. The very adjectives tell us why this form of playwriting is the most popular with the American public outside New York. We are that kind of people, and when we find a play like *Dear Ruth* or *Time Out for Ginger,* we like it in community theatre and in the university and high school productions; and in the case of these particular plays, we also acclaim their Broadway showings. The basic rhythm, in contrast to sophisticated comedy, embraces simplicity, a quality important in everything from the personality types of the actors to the design of the setting most often specified—a living room. Would that more of our best playwrights would try their hands in this form, although many of them are frankly not interested. Not too long ago we saw Sidney Kingsley writing comedy, but his *Lunatics and Lovers* was pointed as directly at the Broadway audience as if it had been *Will Success Spoil Rock Hunter?*

The third general division of comic writing, farce, seems to have a wider appreciation of its rhythm in the English theatre than in ours. Perhaps the austerity of recent English living calls for the broad comedy impact in theatre. The key word of this form is exaggeration. Timing, business, design, and sometimes costume and make-up are broad, underlined, falsely accelerated. There is not much concern with truth or the mirroring of life in farce, the constant objective being the belly laugh. In our own way, and in our younger days as a nation, we paid considerable attention to a native brand of farce which we call burlesque. Although it has disappeared from our stages we can still find high-priced remnants, at times, in the night clubs. We do owe burlesque a very real debt for providing a rugged training ground for many of our finest comic talents. That sort of schooling is no longer available in the American scene.

With melodrama we cross the line toward the more serious writing forms, although its motives, effects, and reasons are often surface affairs. We are speaking of modern works such as *The Desperate Hours* and not of the revivals of the nineteenth century form. I am not too certain that the latter really belongs in a discussion of modern American theatre. For revivals done with fidelity to the old manner we may achieve an interesting museum exhibit, but for the most part, the melodrama revivals are played in a farce manner which results in a theatrical hybrid of questionable parentage, scarcely acceptable within the circle of respectable drama. One day our descendants might present *The Bad Seed* in the farcical manner. I wonder what they would really have?

Modern melodrama has a sharpness of quality which grows as the sense of danger and tensions mount. The director needs to keep his production on exact lines; overdone, the whole point disintegrates. There are interesting ranges in design for this form. Often the bright setting, the pleasant characters, give the extra value of contrast as the plot mounts in tension. Joseph Hayes made the Hilliard family and their home very attractive

so that the white and black contrast with the convicts immediately delivered an exciting emotional impact.

The rhythm of mystery is a projection beyond that of the
darker melodramas. Here the statement of the problem and its
continuance through a maze of wrong turnings and false sus-
picions calls for direction which underlines the key points and
yet keeps plausible the story line. The tension increases as pur-
suit leads to the solution. At times there is opportunity for
rather broad mood treatments in design and lighting although
the normalcy of the settings of *Witness for the Prosecution* also
appeals to writers in this area.

Drama, as a classification, calls for rhythmic treatment of
stature and maturity, which may explain that it lacks the broad
popular appeal of the previous forms. Our premise is that
rhythms of play and audience need to be in rapport. Here are
strong opposing forces and much of the writing is serious, intelligent, and strong. These qualities need reflection in production details. Design is often given an interesting range which
leads to settings like those for *View from the Bridge* and *The
Diary of Anne Frank*. Mood lighting is usually of great help
and can aid the mounting conflict.

Noblest of the play forms in terms of high art is tragedy, not
too often found in current writing. The Greeks, the Elizabethans, and, in this century, the Russians and the Germans
seem to write tragedy more naturally than we do. We are anything but a tragic people and only occasionally do we give popular approval to this dark style. *Death of a Salesman* and *Long
Day's Journey Into Night* have been exceptions rather than the
rule, and their sharp rhythmic contrast in their respective Broadway seasons may have added to their acceptance. While these
examples are not wholly faithful to the stark majesty of an
Oedipus Rex, they are about as close as we are apt to come in

contemporary American playwriting. Here are the noble premises of man against fate and the inevitable march to doom. It is interesting that much of our modern American tragic writing has used characters based in squalor and poverty whereas the Greeks and Shakespeare chose their characters from the purple echelons of gods and royalty.

Within the various groups is still the wide variety of the individual play. Thus the director needs first to find the general rhythmic range and then refine his treatment for the special needs of the manuscript. Through proper timing and exact timerates he can guide his production toward the proper rhythm. Not always will he succeed, but any progress toward the goal will be keeping faith with the principles of creative production.

To check this progress, it is imperative that at the end of the second week the rehearsal schedule alternates detail rehearsals with run-throughs. The first is conducted from the desk onstage, and stops and repeats are the order of work. For the run-throughs the director takes his place in the rear of the auditorium and looks at the entire production using, preferably, all curtains and roughed-in sound and lighting effects. Only in this way can he see how far timing and rhythm have progressed. For these rehearsals, the stage manager keeps exact time-sheets which show not only the running time of each scene but the minutes between. This is of great value as scene and costume changes are rehearsed. With dated time-sheets, it is possible to check the approach to correct running time, and once the play goes into dress rehearsal, the figures ought not to vary more than two or three minutes for the total playing time.

Timing is the pulsation of the play and rhythm is its quality. When they begin to match the dream of the playwright and the conception of the director, then our production is nearing the night when it will be ready to join its audience.

CHAPTER NINE

The Center of Attention

I F WE were to select the most significant element in modern directorial technique, it would be difficult not to choose the center of attention. While long present in the other arts, in some inherently, we do not find it as a conscious part of theatre practice until the twentieth century. That is, it was not used in terms of a production although the stars of yesteryear tried nearly always to retain it as a personal aid. Center-stage, upstage, any advantage of position was sought, or taken, by the star.

The principle, however, is far larger than an individual. The brightest stars of the old days sometimes suffered from its use by a lowly super. In the Opera House of 1890, a leading actress of the day could be reading beautifully the "quality of mercy" speech from "The Merchant." Fifty fellow players could be following the speech in spellbound attention, yet the rankest novice among the walk-ons could destroy the moment. Slowly, and then with increasing enthusiasm, he could begin to grab for an imaginary fly. Within seconds, every eye from the second balcony to the orchestra would be watching him, Portia quite forgotten. If we may believe the stories which have come down to us, not all "fly-catching" was unconscious. It was an inexpensive but stringent revenge exacted by a super who resented the "star."

The center of attention principle is the antithesis of the once-popular move-as-you-feel school of acting. It is based upon a series of physical facts and concludes that at each given moment of a play, the attention of the audience should be focused upon one point of interest. Since only the director can see the entire stage picture, it is he who determines this series of points and then, by direction, inserts them into the production. The difference it has made in the aesthetic pleasure of audiences is tremendous and is reason enough in itself to justify the dominant position of the director in modern theatre.

A clinical exhibit of historical interest comes to us occasionally when television runs the very early movies, those made before 1914. We find these jumpy photographs quite amusing but we do not often question why. It is not that the story lines seem infantile and that most of the acting is overdone, but rather that each foot of film is filled with so much movement that we cannot follow it. Helplessly, we look from one side of the action-filled picture to the other, never being certain what is the point of real interest. Yes, the early movies really moved!

Yet all the while the motion picture possessed the most powerful device yet created to establish and hold the center of attention: the closeup. It was when D. W. Griffith began to bring his camera shot down to the single actor, and still closer, to the actor's face, that movies became the motion pictures and began to grow up.

While this twentieth century contribution to culture quickly solved the basic problem and later passed on the closeup to television, the theatre had to wait twenty-four centuries before it began conscious and consistent use of the principle. This is strange when we realize that the other arts have always counted the center of attention as a basic element of technique.

It is rather simple for the painter to make us look at what he considers the significant element. The scale of most pictures is small enough that we can survey the canvas easily, usually concluding at the center of attention. In the case of a Picasso mural fifty feet in length, the task is not so easy; but even then, the work of the painter is not in motion, so we have all the time we need to find our empathic reaction. The ease with which our gaze moves to Mona Lisa's smile exemplifies the skill with which the masters have used the principle.

The ancient Egyptians, using their cubes and triangles, established the central point, the item of interest, in most of their paintings. In recent times we have seen cubism and expressionism develop beyond the understanding of many an average viewer. In observing an ordinary citizen before an avant garde painting, we may conclude that his dissatisfaction and sense of disturbance come chiefly because he doesn't know what to look at; for him the picture has no center of attention.

So long as sculpture maintained communication with its audience, the principle, again, was easy to apply. There was time to survey the work and to usually find a center of attention. Again, modernism has brought forth some work beyond the appreciation of average viewers but that is a difference in development of viewpoint and not a failure to use the principle. Until now, the writer enjoyed the simplest application of the point of interest, since in his succession of words, phrases, and sentences, he had us looking where he wanted. The current fad of speed reading, racing down the left side of the page at the half-line mark, is disturbing indeed. If the flavor, meaning, and color of words is to be sacrificed in favor of a gluttonous rate of consumption, we may need some revisions in the form.

Music, also, presents no basic difficulty in its form to maintenance of the point of interest. When properly played, the theme, the important phrase, is easy to establish and can proceed directly to the attentive listener. Viewed music is not so simple because of the same physical law which so deeply concerns theatre and the center of attention. Not always does seeing the artist or the orchestra add to the pleasure of the experience. The closed eyes at concerts have a sound aesthetic basis.

It is theatre alone which suffers most from violation of the center of attention and which contains in its basic form many difficulties for its application. First of all, the scale of theatre is large. Our canvas is usually about thirty feet long and ten to fifteen feet high. Unlike our colleagues with cameras, we cannot move in for the tight closeup; all our picture is on view all the time. Further, the continuing elements of our picture are live actors who have to move in our full view when they are on the set. Shakespeare, genius that he was, knew full well that one way to get his audience to listen to an important speech was to take all the other characters off-stage and give his man a soliloquy.

Our cultural satisfactions come mostly through two senses; we do not use tasting, smelling, or touching to any great extent in our enjoyment of the arts. We see and we hear. Unfortunately for theatre, the first of these is more demanding than the second—the visual impression is more dominant than the aural. Our view of the world around us is far more important than the sound of it. When a railroad really wants to safeguard a crossing, it installs red lights; they do the work where bells fail. Diesel locomotives now make their runs with swinging headlights, far more powerful in their warning than all whistles. Most of modern merchandising is based on the authority of sight: we buy the package because we like the way it looks; it is the appearance of the new automobile which sells it, not the sound. The clothing industry depends on our reactions to the appearance of the yearly changes of fashion. Life in the United

States is a wonderful and exciting succession of visual impressions.

This is a hard truth for theatre to face, for in our art form it is the *sound* which has to count most. The aesthetic enjoyment of a play demands that we receive a series of emotional values through spoken words. If this does not happen, then all we see counts for little.

This difficulty would not be quite so overwhelming were it not for the further fact that human vision is a restricted gift. It has prescribed limits. We see clearly only a small circle at any given moment. We have but to look across a room to check this for ourselves. The desk on which we focus comes to us clearly, but as we hold that in view, objects outside that center begin to blur until, on the periphery, they become unrecognizable.

To apply the center of attention principle to living theatre requires that we keep the difficulties constantly in mind. Unlike people in the other arts, we work with a canvas too large to be viewed as a whole. Our living actors provide a constant succession of visual stimuli which will overpower the more essential aural pattern if we permit it. In the auditorium we have hundreds of human eyes which want to follow the central point of interest, but on our canvas they will not know where to look unless we tell them. With the rise of the first curtain the eyes of the audience focus on the stage like hundreds of small spotlight beams, seeing clearly only the center of a limited circle. These beams of vision play about the stage, absorbing the setting and the details of the furnishings. After this moment of general exploration, the beams search for the center of attention. Having come to the play, the audience is ready to believe our story and eager to follow it, but where does the line of meaning begin? Should they continue to regard the girl sitting on the floor reading a book, or watch the lady who is arranging things on the desk across the room? They cannot concentrate their vision on both; they are too far apart. Now the playwright comes to their rescue. A man enters and begins to speak. The girl stops reading and listens to him; the lady turns from the desk to hear his words. With them, the audience focuses its hundreds of vision beams on the man and then sharpens attention on his face. They listen and the play has begun.

From that point until the final curtain, director and actors have to guide the attention of the audience from one center to the next. If we fail to do this, and to do it subtly and efficiently, we have failed our audience and we have failed our play. To direct the constantly moving center of attention so that the audience never loses it but finds the following easy—that is our high directorial objective. At no time can we move them up on the stage to see only the letter on the desk, although the camera closeup can do it with ease. If we want the letter as the point of interest we have to do it with the vast expanse of the setting exposed—a constant source of visual stimuli of varying degrees of interest and color.

We also have living actors placed about that setting. Whenever they move, the audience will concentrate on the movement, for they believe that movement on stage has meaning in the play. Still we have to give the letter the center of attention. Direction solves the problem. As the letter is picked up it becomes the center of attention for every actor on stage. As they concentrate on it and listen to the reading, so does the audience, guided to the point of interest by all the visual elements at the director's command.

This is a potent, but ever fragile, instrument. Halfway through the reading of the letter, a player across stage notices his shoestring untied. He bends down to tie it, and the rapt attention of the audience, which had been on the letter and its

reader, swings at once to the man tying his shoe. The letter
reader might as well stop, for his words will not penetrate the
ears out front; the audience is obeying its natural response to
visual stimuli. In opposition, the aural has no chance. "Fly-catching" did not disappear with the nineteenth century; although
most of it on view today is unconscious, it is no less damaging.

Occasionally a stage exhibition is revealed—they scarcely
deserve to be called plays—which denies all pleasure to its audience by meaningless movement. It is possible to so constantly
destroy the center of attention that the final impression is one
of moving arms and legs, through which very few lines of dialogue ever penetrate. Unless we want to create simply a picture
of motion, as Cecil De Mille does at times with his thousands
of extras filling the screen, this kind of theatrical misbehavior is
unforgivable.

The actors need a sound understanding of the idea if the
director is to use it in full effectiveness. Appreciation of the
principle can be established by example. Ask the company to sit
in the auditorium and watch a two-person scene. First have them
check on the narrow diameter of complete vision as they follow
the action from one side of the stage to the other. Then either
take out a piece of business which destroys the speech of the
other actor or insert such a bit of business for illustration. There
is an advantage in following a briefing on the subject with such
a demonstration.

The first step is to be certain that all movement in the play
belongs and is necessary. This is a matter for directorial decision; once more, only he sees the whole picture, as it is developing and as he wants it in fulfillment. To speed the work, he
asks the actors to analyze their movement patterns and see if
there are any visual actions which have no meaning. If actions

are unfounded in a reason, they are probably extraneous and should be eliminated.

There are a number of conventional actions which lie somewhat outside this general rule. They include such processes as eating, knitting, sewing, card playing, and other continued actions called for by playwrights. Even these need careful scrutiny. In one scene of *It's Never Too Late,* we found that Granny's knitting action blurred a scene although it was a device which the character used frequently. At several key moments it was necessary for her to stop knitting and turn her full attention to the lines being spoken around her. At once, the scenes were clarified.

Knowing that sound is almost invariably subordinate to sight, the general rule is that the speaker is the center of attention. Not often is a movement on one side of the stage more important than the speech being given on the other. It can happen when the *reaction* is the point of interest. This is common camera technique, used when the face of the listening character is shown while the speaker is off-camera. In theatre we have the rather involved problem of giving the character in reaction such a strong visual position that the audience will stay with him.

There is also the matter of the cross which continues after completion of the line. It is sometimes possible to correct this by shortening the distance or respacing the reading to cover the time needed. Even the lines of motion involved in getting up and sitting can blur the point of interest. A beginner in theatre can hardly believe that an audience will continue to follow a character while he gets completely into the chair, but audiences are ever subject to the dominance of visual stimuli. As with crosses, corrections can often be made by retiming the reading or accelerating the rate of movement.

It would seem that in most cases only the speaker is in motion. What, then, do the other players on stage do? The general answer is nothing, *except:* to listen effectively and with the illusion of the first time; to remain absolutely in character; to react inwardly and completely; and to continue the emotional creative line. Facial reaction needs to be limited to the point that it does not demand attention in itself, save in the exceptions we have mentioned, when *it* is the center of attention. This scarcely simple complex of physical and emotional demands will give answer and comfort to the players who ask, "What do I do in the long spaces between my speeches?"

When this is understood and put into practice, there will be a noticeable tightening up of the play. Now the full energies of every on-stage actor are involved one hundred percent of the time. Between his own speeches he is building the scene by his inward emotional and mental reactions. By his listening he builds the listening of the audience; and the finer his illusion of the first time, the finer will be theirs. By remaining in character and continuing the emotional creative line he is ready to pick up his cue exactly and read his speech with the directed visual pattern connected with it. At that moment *he* becomes the center of attention: the spotlighted portion of a picture of which he had been a subordinate part.

In many plays there are moments when the effect desired is of general reaction: the startling announcement, the arrival of a new character, the rare comedy line written to amuse the characters as such. For these the director sets reactions and movements which belong to the character and allows the center of attention to diffuse in a general effect. To pull this diffusion back into sharp focus on the next point of interest calls for careful timing and exact teamwork by the actors in the scene.

A typical example is the second-act mind-reading scene in *The Great Sebastians.* As Essie, seated blindfolded at the desk right, takes the questions from the bowl and "reads" them, the twelve actors grouped at left react with group lines and growing astonishment. The trickiest point in the scene concerned the center of attention when Essie substituted the previously read question for the next one in the bowl. It was essential for the audience to see this minute piece of business although General Zandek's group of guests across the stage could not be allowed to see it. It was simple enough for Rudi to send the group's attention into the hall as he strode up left center demanding, "Is there someone out there!" The difficulty was in getting the audience to turn attention back to Essie at the desk. The answer was with Rudi, who occupied that always strong stage position of one against the crowd. At the exact moment when the group became quiet as they peered into the hall, he turned his head and body toward Essie. This guided the audience to the new point of interest quite as effectively as a magician does when he makes you look at the wrong hand while the other does the trick. As soon as Rudi had transferred the beam of attention to Essie, she began to exchange the folded pieces of paper and the line of movement, no longer than six inches, was picked as efficiently out of the thirty by eighteen foot stage picture as if the director had been able to say to the cameraman, "Make this a tight closeup."

Color is an important device for underlining the importance of a character, with many degrees of emphasis possible through choice of shade and intensity. Decisions about costume colors need to be weighed carefully, since it is possible to so dress a subordinate role that it will have an undue visual importance. White is most powerful in its impact and costumes in that color are not to be lightly assigned. Directors have wondered why a minor actor seemed so important visually when he did nothing more than take off his jacket and play the scene in a white shirt.

It is difficult for an audience to draw its attention from a white area on a stage. Well-designed costume plots give full recognition to color values and scale their selections to the director's decisions as to relative importance.

When controlled lighting was added to the tools of the theatre, the director was given another strong instrument connected with the center of attention principle. The brighter areas of a setting exert a constant demand for attention which the director coordinates with important speeches and scenes. One of the earliest examples of using light to establish a point of interest was the old follow-spot, still stock equipment for the vaudeville performer. There were once productions of straight dramas which followed the star through the entire performance with a balcony spotlight. Since some of those early units were of the blazing carbon arc variety, the point of interest did not move far from the brightly illuminated star so long as he or she was on stage. Now we use stage lighting more subtly, knowing that both intensity and gelatine colors can be used for added emphasis.

As work proceeds toward clarifying the point of interest through the entire production, the director will find how sound his judgments were about floor plans and the construction details of the settings. If the most important entrances are made from a door which is not in a strong visual position, some drastic revision of direction may be required to compensate for the weakness. Corrections are possible through all the elements of production: position, lighting, color, time, and the others.

As we neared dress rehearsals on *The Desperate Hours* we found that the scene in the upstairs bedroom between Mr. Hilliard and his son Ralphie was not sufficiently solidified as the center of attention, although they were playing it well. At that point there are several other characters on-stage—on the stair

and in the downstairs living room. Even with all of them adding to the point of interest by bodily positions turned toward
the door of the upstairs room, attention was still diffused. We
then found that by increasing the intensity of the light in the
bedroom and bringing down slightly the other areas, our beam
of attention from the auditorium would hold at the proper point.

Ways to fidelity to the principle are as various as the possibilities of direction and technical facilities. The essential matter is
that the director and his cast fully understand the importance of
the technique and hold firm to each step of progress toward the
realization. A clearly defined center of attention gives a clarity to
the play; it becomes easy to watch. This in itself is an important
move toward proper empathy. Confusion in visual impact makes
an audience restless. Not knowing where to look has the same
deadly result as not being able to hear. But when the opening
of a production moves smoothly and accurately, with the center
of attention constantly established, rapport between players and
audience begins.

Now the playwright's story line comes through clearly, its
values heightened by being the continuing point of interest. In
community theatres this has solid value, for the play itself makes
a balanced impression. Our center of attention is not distorted
by the presence of a star's virtuoso talent demanding constant
interest for itself. Our concern is with the play, and by our
technique we are giving it every opportunity. The result is apt
to be different from the Broadway performance—not necessarily
better but different. We are not selling a star. The brilliance of
his or her performance will not be a factor on our stage, for we
are dedicated to the play. So often community theatres hear,
"You know, we saw the same show in New York, but we liked
the play better here." They may not have said the word in italics
but we know what they mean. The *play* may have had a better
chance. It is a worthy reason for any theatre.

CHAPTER TEN

End of Prompting—Mutual Emotional Experience

A SIGNIFICANT point in the rehearsal schedule is reached with the end of prompting. Until now we have been absorbed in learning the play and mastering various steps of technique. Now, in a single rehearsal, we change our objective to a higher level. Our experience has found that a reasonable date for this transition is six nights before the opening. Two weeks earlier, the director announces the end of prompting and follows that with several reminders. The knowledge that after this time the crutch of the prompter's voice will be removed is a good psychological spur to rapid learning. If a group is applying the idea for the first time there may be some concern, but once the worth is proved, there is a new pride and dignity thrown about the organization's concept of acting.

In twenty-seven years—nearly two hundred productions and nearly two thousand performances—we have never given a prompt. The talent involved in these productions has been typical of any community theatre group: the beginners, the experienced, and those who have previously worked under the prompting system. That it can be practiced over such a length of time and with a heterogeneous group numbering hundreds of players is a sound argument for its applicability.

Our abhorrence of the prompter's voice began long before we started our careers. In childhood, our playgoing was marred by the frequent intrusion of the off-stage voice. It is possible to recall actors, paid for their work, who would stand on a stage and call, "Line!" With such exhibitions of inadequacy, all creativity succumbed and the theatre was no longer a place of wonder and excitement but only an auditorium and a stage peopled by those undeserving of the privilege.

Giving acting this adjunct of dignity has nothing to do with the physical qualifications of the performance site. It works equally well in the school auditorium, on an improvised platform, or in a fully equipped playhouse. Indeed, to work without a prompter is a hallmark of which any producing organization can be proud.

But two fundamentals are required for its use: sound preparation of all the steps to this point and a full understanding of its reason. All that we have learned—blocking, memorization, characterization, listening and projection, concentration, timing and rhythm, and the center of attention—these are the foundation stones of our final objective, creative acting. Unless we now move toward that artistic goal, our play may be technically sound but emotionally dull, a creature which moves and talks in directed patterns but with all the shortcomings of a mechanical man. Such a coldly structural form is not likely to win the hearts and minds of the audience.

At the critique of the rehearsal the night before, the director explains the procedure of the end-of-prompting rehearsal. For the one night, the words of the playwright, which have been the subject of so much study, are no longer of great concern. Naturally they are the best choices to express the ideas and emotions, for the author labored long to find them; but now we are going to place the meaning and emotional values of the play ahead of the actual text. If the end-of-prompting rehearsal is faithful to meaning and emotion, then it will be a success although there may be substitution of occasional words. The actors are not to be concerned about any line difficulties; they have more important points of concentration. The assistant stage manager will record line errors on a simple form which lists the characters and opposite their names the number of the page on which the difficulty happened. In the script the offending line is checked. After rehearsals, for this system continues, it is easy for the actor to find where he erred and note it in his own sides.

Since human memories are not infallible, the no-prompting plan implies that responsibility is mutual. Every actor in a scene is responsible for the life of that scene. It is not unlike the conduct of a good football team. They are taught not to fumble but occasionally this mishap does occur. It would be a very strange group of athletes who would see their left halfback drop the ball and then stand back saying, "It was his fumble, let *him* pick it up."

So it is with alert, well-trained actors. A slight deviation from the exact text, a slow cue, even a twisted sentence, can not be allowed to damage the continuity of the scene. This might seem to demand a sound knowledge of all the lines of each scene in which a player appears, and it does precisely that. The exact *words* are not essential, but the exact *meaning* is. The audience has no libretto to follow and cares not if a word or two is changed; but it cares if the flow of the play is stopped, and resents the destruction of all the created values which happens when the voice of a prompter is heard from the wings.

Obviously, asking such responsibility of actors steps up their degree of concentration. Now they know they can allow nothing to come between them and the play. The added concentration has many benefits which are far from being fringe, not the least of which is the subtle completion of characterization. That intricate process which began two weeks before, when we were saying "If I were. . . ," has now grown until the process of identification with the role is almost automatic; the early gradations of assimilation have been bypassed by the technique which has come with practice.

This fits perfectly into the plan. As added concentration makes for more complete characterization, the purposes of that character become more prominent in all the mental and physical actions of the actor. Now he will begin to be impelled to complete the reasons for his presence in each scene. There will be a new driving force which will sharpen all the coordinating processes, thereby improving the exactness of memorization and all the other learned steps of technique. As any psychologist will agree, this building of purpose and strengthening of basic drives is the surest way to avoid any sense of stage fright—which is chiefly the result of paying attention to the wrong things and which in turn has a diffusive effect on learned processes.

The extra tension, as actual performance nears, is a normal result of the situation; like the athlete, the actor gains from the adrenalin increase. It gives the extra vitality which is often the margin of difference between an average performance and a brilliant one. Fear of the experience, one of the definitions of stage fright, can be eliminated in the novice as well as the veteran by sound progression through rehearsal, and by so well establishing the *purposes* of each character that *they* remain the motivating objectives.

Our rehearsal timetable is based on a minimum of twenty full rehearsals: five each week for the first two weeks, and ten consecutive sessions. The last six rehearsals before the opening are the period of creative realization. To use this time to its fullest, every effort should be made to conduct them on a performance basis. Many groups are not able to enjoy this advantage, since their performances are given in rented auditoriums. In many cases only one or two nights of rehearsal on stage are possible, but this need not destroy all the advantages of performance simulation for the last six nights. An example of how extreme this problem can be is illustrated by a community theatre group in one of our large southern cities. Their only housing is in the school system but they are not allowed on the stage until seven o'clock on the night of performance. To add to the travail, the set or settings have to be cleared from the stage after the performance and reassembled the next night for the second of the two performances! Yet in spite of these hardships, this group follows the general plan of creative realization for the last six rehearsals.

In their simple quarters, they are able to use their setting for this period. Scene changes are rehearsed so that the move to the performance stage finds the crew fully prepared. The long delays for scene changes have almost disappeared from the noncommercial theatre and should certainly not be allowed to destroy the evening's pleasure for the audience. While this group has no curtain in its rehearsal hall, the use of blackouts provides accurate timing for scenes and acts. Most of the time, the actual furniture and final properties are available during the week. Make-up can always be brought into the production at the proper time, regardless of the housing facilities. The actual costumes are used, starting with the first of four dress rehearsals.

Too often groups without their own buildings use that fact as an excuse for not trying to perfect as many of the technical factors as possible. The result is an attempt to bring them together in one or two frantic last nights of preparation, which is completely unfair to the actors and the play. Small wonder that such productions contain so little creative acting; it is remarkable that the players find their way through the maze of new technical circumstances.

Even more to be criticized are the organizations showing in their own plants who fail to give the play a fair chance during this final stage of development. In their cases, these six rehearsals ought to be complete run-throughs with nothing allowed to stop concentration upon the performance. If adjustments are still needed for certain lighting units, let them be done before or after the run-through. A rearrangement of properties, a costume alteration, a slow curtain—these and all technical details are of minor importance. Their correction cannot be allowed to stop the play.

For now we are concerned with the greatest element of theatre, its reason for existence: mutual emotional experience. Here is the central flame of the entire idea. When it burns brightly, nothing else is really important. If it dims, or goes out, the finest of playhouses and the most elegant scenery are but grim reminders that true theatre is, and has always been, a communion of emotional experience between actors and audience. It was happening when the citizens of Athens sat on the hillside to watch the plays; it continued through the dark centuries when theatre survived on the tiny islands of the church steps, and through the miracle and mystery plays; it was lusty and robust during the time of the Elizabethans; and it continues through the performances which are really significant tonight.

Part of the wonder of it all is that theatre alone offers this emotional rapport as the complete group experience. The other arts use the principle but in diverse and less powerful forms. The painter's creative experience is a solitary emotion, separated from that of the viewer by space and time. The sculptor is also alone in his creativity; the writer works in solitude. Jotting down the notes on paper, the composer knows not when his creative emotion will find reflection in an audience. For all of these there is the bittersweet satisfaction of thinking that though the contemporary world may not appreciate them, one day an audience of sufficient quality may evolve. Even the musician in performance is having a *personal* creative experience. We cannot share it with him; we can but drink in the sound and then, when the music is over, express thanks for our own personal experiences by applauding.

Only the actor, who is his own instrument, creates emotional experience which cannot be preserved but has to be shared *at the moment* with an audience in living theatre. Only when the actors and audience are present at the same point of time *and* in the same place, can this emotional communion occur. This rules out the mechanical media, where the experiences are separated by time and space or both.

The motion picture form has a long and rich heritage and the talented men and women of the industry continually strive to surpass themselves. Certainly the fine players involved undergo the experience of creativity. With the general objective of completing two minutes of satisfactory film each shooting day, the emotional values of a particular scene often reach great heights. Because a motion picture is usually made in pieces and not in sequence, the created emotion lacks the wholeness of that enjoyed by the actor on the stage, who has to play the entire written life span of the character at every performance.

Still more significant, from our viewpoint, is that the motion picture player has no personal contact with his audience. Somewhere ahead, those audiences will gather in the darkened movie house and the finished film will unroll. Whether the group numbers two or two thousand will not affect the speed nor the sound of the talking picture. They may munch their popcorn, laugh, or cry; their actions will not affect the images on the screen. There is no point of human contact. Together the audiences seem to have a joint experience; yet, because of the impersonality of the machines between them and the actors, that experience more closely resembles the individual one of each person at a musical event. It is even less a group experience, for the movie audience does not have the privilege of joint applause at the performance end. There is no real thread connecting the individuals of the motion picture audience save their presence in the same auditorium.

There are some in Hollywood who think the motion picture would gain by increased use of theatre-like presentation—perhaps two showings a day with intermission. This would improve the feeling of group unity, because all would arrive and leave together and the best pictures might begin to win their oft-deserved applause; but here the approach to theatre ends. Certainly any development of audience response by the motion picture would be a gain for theatre. Fifty years of the silver screen have dulled the emotional abilities of the American public. There are many who, after a lifetime of movie going and a decade of television, forget on their occasional visits to theatre that positive emotional response, with its audible components of laughter and applause, is a very real part of the theatre experience.

For most of the same reasons, television is denied the privilege of common emotional experience with its audience. Even "live" productions and studio audiences cannot change the fact that the actor and his real audience, dispersed through millions of living rooms, are so separated by space that the emotional response of the one cannot directly affect the emotional experience of the other.

Is mutual emotional experience, possessed only by theatre among the arts, so vital, so important? Is it the continuing reason for theatre's existence through twenty-five centuries? Does it seem powerful enough to insure continuance through the mechanical wonder-ages ahead?

In answering these questions affirmatively, we recognize that it is imperative that we so teach our players that they will fully appreciate this basic, vital, and continuing element of living theatre. All the other *parts* of theatre can be done better in other media. It is a costly and inefficient way in which to preach ideas or credos. The podium and the press are far better suited. As a story-telling device, it cannot vie with the short story or the novel in the cost of reaching a vast audience. As a medium of mass entertainment it cannot compete with the motion picture, radio, or television. The economics of theatre are ridiculous by comparison. For two hundred thousand dollars, television can present *The Great Sebastians* with Alfred Lunt and Lynn Fontanne in *one* night to an audience of fifty million. Not only that, but it was given to that vast audience free, the production costs paid happily by sponsors who felt full value in their commercials. To present that one play to theatre audiences, paying but two dollars a ticket and numbering a million a year, would cost that free television audience one hundred million dollars and the process would consume a half-century!

Obviously, theatre is like no other business. But can we not justify living theatre as a place of high intellectual transport? No; music and poetry are among the art forms which provide this highly personal experience much more satisfactorily. Perhaps we ought to consider it more as a place of visual beauty and spectacle. Again, the earthbound stage cannot compete with the simplest motion picture, and the widest screens and the newest color processes make the best of stage settings seem puny and drab. We may say that the pageant of the playhouse is made of *living* people, but we lose again as we regard the scale, even majesty, of sports contests in the great stadiums and arenas. And the forty, sixty, or eighty thousand fans yelling their football team on or rooting for their favorite boxer are also enjoying that rare portion of living—mutual emotional experience. However, the range of the fan's emotion goes no higher than the empathic delight of seeing the football moved across the goal line or the fighter knock his opponent down for the full count.

When a group of people seek this pleasure among the higher emotions, they can find it only in theatre. Here are brought together all the factors which theatre does second-best, in a resultant combination found only on the living stage. And then the wonderful ingredient: actors who are alive at the same time and place as the audience and who, in their generosity, will act the play again for each new audience.

This is splendid, but it is not all. For encompassing the whole process, transmuting the simple elements into a special and excellent whole, is this unique element of the living theatre, mutual emotional experience.

In treating this subject we cannot continue to a philosophical discussion of a truly theatric approach to life, although it might logically follow. I feel, with many others, that Robert Edmond Jones has given us a beautifully clear, idealistic treatment of this in his superb *The Dramatic Imagination*.

Our concern is to give the average director a frame of reference for mutual emotional experience from which he can give his players an understanding of its essential value. We have found that one or two briefing sessions, using the material above, has given our people a sound respect for the principle. Even beginners, once they begin to grasp the implications, seem to move ahead to an approach to creative acting. When the entire company understands and believes in this central reason for existence, the play has a chance to complete its development through the final rehearsals.

Creative acting *can* happen if the progressive steps have been well learned. Concentration upon living through the emotional pattern of the play will fill out the characterizations and bring adeptness at using the points of technique. The director may not have to mention daily study so often; incentive should be increasing.

If these conditions prevail, there should be a feeling of readiness, almost an eagerness, to join with an audience. This is clearly stated in our word "mutual," for not until the audience is present can there be communion of emotion.

This bringing together of play and audience is not an easy transition; a learning experience of some magnitude is not only implied but inherent. Broadway knows this well and gives its companies the benefit of several weeks in the tryout cities. The commercial theatre has, of course, the added problem of adjusting and rewriting a new manuscript to eliminate as many faults as possible before it opens in New York.

The noncommercial theatre, for the most part, works with tested plays and is thus free of manuscript treatment. However, even one week of tryout performances is rarely feasible. In the most favorable situations, the most that can be managed are one or two preview audiences. These, we feel, are essential.

To ask a nonprofessional company to open a production with no audience experience before the first night is unfair. The cast needs some knowledge of reaction, a foretelling of possible laughs, a reasonable chance to experience the mutuality of emotion.

Organizations which have never used the preview audience may well find it one of the most valuable additions to the production schedule. Instead of asking players, many of whom may be beginners, to face their first audience on opening night, we need to remove this emotional and psychological threat to creativity—for it can be that. We have found it wise to bring play and the first preview audience together at the first of the four dress rehearsals.

CHAPTER ELEVEN

Dress Rehearsals and Opening Night

Our steps of technique have been based on a rehearsal schedule of twenty working nights. Some groups will want more than this and there are advantages in a longer learning time. But whether we rehearse our play twenty, thirty, or forty times, no four sessions have more potential value than those devoted to dress rehearsal. This evaluation is pertinent, since this is the part of preparation most often abused. We have stressed that unless the group adheres to a timetable of production steps, there will come a time of reckoning; settlement will surely arrive with dress rehearsals.

Of the countless occupations, professions, and crafts with which Americans today fill their working hours, few are as subject to damage from procrastination as play production. In the factory, failure to turn a bolt on a moving item does not close the plant. The unit can be removed for correction. If the carpenter fails to complete the siding today, the house is not wrecked. If the trucker is late with his delivery at the station, it does not damage the railroad.

Play production is different. Here failure to complete any of the countless jobs *on time* may damage, even destroy, the object of the entire effort. It is not enough to work twice as fast at the wrong time, as we learned when we considered the step of memorization. Yet this is what happens with countless groups, usually during that last vital period of preparation, the dress rehearsals. Here in a last frenzied effort to make amends for procrastination the painters dab furiously, the electricians connect and set lights, the costumers scurry, and the make-up people wonder what colors they should use. Perhaps the stage crew decides it is time to find how the settings change, and several good but tardy souls search frantically for the final properties.

The picture is not a caricature; there have been, and still are, dress rehearsals like that. During such chaotic proceedings there is one forgotten element: the play. There may be some consciousness that all the noisy undertakings are related to the central project, but hardly ever realization that by their very presence at the wrong time in the schedule irreparable harm may be done. At the time when the play should be coming to final development with its first test audience, it is battered by late technical completion.

I think that we misunderstand the real meaning of the ancient adage, "The show must go on." There is a larger and more important concept than the ill actor struggling through his part, or the suddenly alerted understudy covering himself with glory. It is splendid that the people of theatre have always taken their obligation to their audiences so seriously as to try to complete all announced performances, but it doesn't have to happen. The world will not stop if a play misses a showing. The public very graciously accepts "technical difficulties" in other entertainment media.

For me, the grand old phrase implies that the living theatre is such a splendid example of civilized man's ability to express himself in a group art form that all who are privileged to be connected with a production will be impelled to do their work at the proper time so that their "show will go on" enjoying every aid and facility for its success. If more groups worked with this interpretation, the quality of play production would move so sharply upward that a grateful public would not mind if occasionally a performance or two was cancelled by emergency situations.

Another traditional phrase should no longer be allowed in the jargon of theatre. A bad dress rehearsal does *not* mean a good performance. The origin of this misstatement is lost in antiquity but it was probably first spoken as an excuse for dilatoriness. It may have been that some Renaissance entrepreneur who forgot to get the scenery ready on time and who had actors who were under-rehearsed and costumers who put off their work faced the whole scrambled mess at a dress rehearsal. Then a minor miracle happened and the next night the performance went reasonably well. Perhaps he then spoke the fatal words which have been a blot on the escutcheon of the theatre ever since. It is too late for us to tell *him* the real truth but the rest of us should know it. When a good performance occurs after a bad dress rehearsal it is due either to sheer luck or a benevolent providence.

We now know that a play is a fragile creation subject to the frailties and faults of many human and technical factors. When all of these are in splendid condition and every point on the timetable has been met, there is still a formidable task in bringing the play to life before its audience. The dress rehearsals of a play are a special time. There may be various activities before and after the running of the dress rehearsals but from the first curtain to the last, nothing is as important as the play. It is harmful to stop between scenes for extensive alterations, adjustments, or corrections of technical factors. The sense of momentum and continuity, to say nothing of creativity, calls for dress rehearsals running on performance time and schedule. We have underlined our insistence that technical elements be added to a production at stated points on the timetable but occasionally a group will follow this sound plan and then have difficulty with the human element.

Watching a final dress rehearsal of a young community theatre, I felt pleased with the play and emotional values as they built through the first act and the initial scene of the second. Then as the curtain was about to rise on the next scene, the electrician shouted to "hold it." Dragging his tallest ladder to center stage, he announced that he had to reset a light. Having climbed to the unit, he decided to change the connection, all the while carrying on a monologue. After almost fourteen minutes, he pulled his ladder off-stage, obviously delighted to have had his moment of attention. Finally the curtain rose but it was not the same play. The actors, who had worked so hard and so well, were completely out of time, character, and purpose. They were nearly through the scene before there was any semblance of life in the play. And all for want of a spotlight adjustment! I did not see the performance on the following night but I venture that it was not quite so good as it might have been had one technical adjustment not been allowed to stop the dress rehearsal.

Of course we want the silent, visual aids—the scenery, properties, lights, costumes, and make-up—to be right. But directors and technicians need always to remember a precept of theatre practice: after an audience has applauded a setting at the rise of the curtain, it will not find mutual emotional experience in the settings, the furnishings, or the fanciest of lighting. What the audience wants can be found only in the play.

We have found no better way to insure the uninterrupted flow of the first dress rehearsal and to give the actors the feel of audience experience than to provide a small test audience at this time. It holds many advantages.

For groups in their own buildings, the only new technical additions for this performance are full costumes and make-up. Both of these are subject to the exceptions that when there is intricacy or complication, more rehearsals are needed. When costumes are rented they often are not available for more than the four dress rehearsals, but simulated dress for a number of earlier rehearsals will cut down the hazards of at last putting the actresses into hoop skirts or the men into uniforms.

An apparently minor point in costuming can cause trouble if under-rehearsed. All quick changes should be thoroughly worked out so that by dress rehearsal time there is no margin for error. The creativity of players can be as completely destroyed by a sudden costume problem as by that electrician on top of his ladder cracking jokes and setting lights. Each costume change, with all accessories, needs to be listed by the player's dressing room mirror, so that a glance will give the answer and eliminate one more chance for confusion. Many actors like to have the properties they use in each scene added to the costume list—a simple but useful device to aid our general objective of keeping players' minds free for concentration on their essential work.

College and high school productions have few obstacles in following the four dress rehearsals plan, and many do follow it. In the secondary schools it has a special value in giving stability and confidence to the young players. For the community groups who have to rehearse in one location and give performances in another, the idea is not easy to follow but there are possible compromises.

If there is any way to work in the finished setting for the last week it should be done. This requires early completion but the setting ought not to be too difficult to set up in the rehearsal quarters, since its portability is already specified. As we have said, if this is not feasible, working in the actual performance furniture will be helpful. The lighting presents a real difficulty, since the groups usually employ the equipment of the rented auditorium. Even here, an important safeguard is to have several light rehearsals under the director's supervision at the auditorium. If the units are close to position and all cues are understood and rehearsed, lighting can be fitted to the play in one or two nights without distraction to the actors.

Certainly the properties, costumes, and make-up can be worked in the simplest of surroundings. If the group has only a room for rehearsal, mastering this much of the technical side will be of inestimable help in making the move to the performance auditorium.

There is wide variation in the attitude of school authorities toward community drama. In many cities the cooperation is excellent, and in some new school construction, little theatres to be shared with community activities are part of the building plan. In many situations, the real need is that superintendents and school boards understand the high value of community theatre as one of the most potent aids to adult education in its best and broadest sense. This will take time, but it is happening.

The small test audience at the first dress rehearsal is so beneficial that even the groups who cannot move to their performance stage at that point should employ the device. The number can be small—twenty or thirty will do—but they should be persons not close to the organization nor members of the regular audience. We have always combined the need for this small audience with the opportunity to invite those who would not otherwise see the play. The pattern has been to ask, in turn, such groups as the clergy, servicemen, and when the play is suitable, children from an orphans' home. Every town has those who would delight in the opportunity to see a play but who would not likely be present except by the invitation to the private performance.

The time of the first dress rehearsal will vary with performance. For us it occurs on Sunday afternoon, as we open on Thursday nights to take advantage of two weekends during the run. This also gives the company a full night away from rehearsal with a chance to get needed rest.

But whenever it takes place and in whatever housing, the procedure needs to follow as exactly as possible a real performance. The stage manager from this point on makes the conventional calls of "half hour" and "fifteen minutes." At ten minutes before curtain, he calls the company together for the briefing. For men and women who earn their livings by acting, there may be no need for a talk from the director before each dress rehearsal and performance; for amateur players it is not only psychologically helpful, but provides the most efficient way of communicating last minute announcements and points of procedure. Athletic coaches know well the value of their final talks to the team before the game, and an astute director can send his company into performance in the proper frame of mind.

Points to be covered include: a reminder to the crew to double check every item and to be certain that the stand-by mechanical equipment is working and ready; a request that actors check the on-stage properties they use to be certain they are in position, and that the property crew have actors show them all props being carried in pockets, handbags, and briefcases; and a reminder that the no-smoking rule, which now goes into effect for the entire stage area and continues to the end of the run, has to be rigidly enforced.

If the play has laugh lines, point out that now begins the learning of one of the most pleasant items of the actors' technique: waiting for laughs. While the small audience will not give a loud response, any reaction will be indicative. A full audience laugh is shaped like a wave, ascending in an increasing curve and dropping back to silence. The dialogue should be continued slightly before the laugh ends. There is a moment when the actor can be heard, and speech should begin again at that point, to avoid the break in continuity which happens if silence is allowed to follow a laugh. When a speech has begun and a laugh interrupts it, the actor has two obligations. The first is to continue reacting in character (if not overdone, this may quite properly increase the laugh) until he can be heard. He has also to decide at what point the line was covered by the audience's reaction and continue his speech from there. It is wrong to repeat any part of a speech which has already been heard. The director may honestly add that while this may sound like an intricate reaction pattern to be so quickly learned, it is not difficult and the very beginners in the cast will be practicing it quite well by the second or third performance.

Finally, the director points out that, at last, they are reaching the objective of all the work and preparation. As players and audience meet and the crew provides the technical atmosphere and effect, the play begins to come to life. If each will concentrate completely and execute exactly his rehearsed assignment for the next two hours, it will be an exciting and satisfactory experience. With the request for "Places, please," the director moves to the auditorium. He fills in the program details for the audience group and asks that they enlarge their responses to make up for their numbers. As he takes his place in the rear of the auditorium where he can make notes on his clipboard, the first dress rehearsal begins.

Primary objective of the second dress rehearsal is to enlarge the audience with its many connotations. Again the invited list ought not to come from the organization nor include any potential members of the regular audiences. A source for this second preview group is readily found in the school system. In our case, we invite the five high schools, in rotation, to send their dramatic clubs and speech and drama students. Faculty members accompany the students and furnish lists of those expected. Even at this point on the timetable it is important to rigidly maintain the "no visitors" rule.

The briefing starts with a review of any errors in the first dress rehearsal, and notes all changes in technical procedure. These will likely be minor details such as rearrangement of furniture storage off-stage to add to the speed of a scene change. Perhaps one or two of the make-ups need adjustment as to color or intensity. If the preparation plan has been well executed and on time there ought not to be many corrections. The second audience experience is the chief target of the evening, and with a student group which may number from forty to seventy-five, more definite laughs can be expected if the play contains them. It is well to call for a curtain twenty to thirty minutes earlier than the regular performance time so that the company can get a little extra rest. With the announcement that on the next night the company will be allowed to watch the play as their time permits, the director retires to the auditorium to greet the audience, give program notes, and observe the rehearsal.

There is an interesting reaction when the third dress rehearsal returns the production to the complete possession of the company after they have shared it twice with preview audiences. When the company is reminded that once the play opens, it belongs to the public and they can no longer see it from the auditorium, there is a new appreciation of the privilege of sitting out front. It is important, of course, for the company to realize that watching does not lessen the obligation to be backstage in good time for all entrances or crew duties. The briefing covers the previous night's work and notes any errors or corrections. If the straight make-ups have been learned satisfactorily, they may be omitted from this rehearsal. Any make-up which changes the appearance has to be executed nightly, since it is upsetting to actors, accustomed to playing to a character make-up, not to have the correct visual surroundings. With the statement that time between scenes is to be kept to the absolute minimum and that curtain calls will be rehearsed after the play, the director again goes to the auditorium to check the run-through.

For the two preview audiences, a simple straight-line curtain call will suffice, but in preparation for opening night this detail needs to be carefully worked out. An excellent noncommercial production need not conclude with careless or awkward curtain calls, which differ unnecessarily from professional productions where they are done so well.

Some educational theatres and a few community groups either do not take curtain calls or limit them to the uninteresting, straight-line company bow. We cannot agree, for the curtain call, well done, can be a graceful conclusion to an evening of living theatre. The mechanical media do not have this privilege, although at times the television actors will appear after the play. They are denied, however, the favorite sound of actors—the applause of an appreciative audience.

Some directors feel that it does not reflect the democratic atmosphere of community theatre, but there is larger sentiment for the interest which can be built by variation of curtain calls. While the philosophy of community theatre includes the precept that each player is important, and the result of that attitude has many benefits to the play, it does not seem unfair to scale the curtain calls to the size of respective roles. Most casts will fall into four units, beginning with the shorter parts and concluding with the leading characters. I do agree that educational and community theatre should rarely have a curtain call for an individual. This is too close to the star system. For the two or four longest parts to be assigned to the third or fourth call, however, does not seem discriminatory.

A basic form is to bring in the first unit, have them bow at center, and then take their places at either side at the front of the set. On the second curtain, the second unit enters and bows, while the first four players stand at attention. Then they move to positions on the line while the third unit enters and is acknowledged. This gives each unit of actors one curtain, and when all are in, presents a line across the stage. The next call has the whole company bowing in unison. All bows are better if made on a count, perhaps of five, being down on three and up on five. If there is another call, it is graceful for the players to nod and smile at the audience rather than to take another bow.

There are endless variations: the taking of hands when the line is formed, the short step together toward the curtain, and the "picture call," which fits certain plays. "Jenny Kissed Me" ends on a happy note which suggests that Father Moynihan may continue to improve the appearance of the students, as he has so successfully done with Jenny. We evolved a series of calls which brought in first the high school girls with their carryalls. As they took their places on one side of the setting, Father Moynihan, in pantomime, began explaining the beauty hints. As the calls continued, the rest of the cast, in units, came in to observe. It made a hit with the audiences and gave a pleasant feeling of extension to a happy performance.

The fourth and final dress rehearsal has two objectives: to rehearse the play a last time, and to get the company home early. For groups who have but one night on a rented stage, this is asking a great deal; yet it is important that actors are not overtired for their opening. Most of the frenzy and confusion of some dress rehearsals comes from the technical side. If actors can be spared late dress rehearsals by sacrificing scenic and lighting effects, sacrifice them. I do not remember meeting anyone who ever bought theatre tickets to look at scenery or lighting, but I recall nights of great theatre where there was not much on the stage but well-directed players. Those who can recall the tours of the Abbey Theatre may have forgotten how worn and decrepit were the pathetic settings, but most of us will never forget the radiant performances which happened in front of them.

There are no figures extant but we may hope that most non-commercial groups have the privilege of at least two dress rehearsals on the performance stage. In their cases, any necessary confusion of moving in and setting up should be confined to the first night and the play should have complete dominance the second night. It is too late for the fundamentals. Blocking, characterization, listening, projection, line reading, timing, rhythm, and the center of attention—these have to be studied and mastered before dress rehearsals begin. The football team does not work on blocking and tackling the night before the game.

Two essentials belong in all dress rehearsal briefings: intensifying of concentration and the creation of mutual emotional experience. If these are achieved, all the points of technique will fall into the rehearsed pattern. The optimistic director who has done his work well can raise morale by commenting on the good work being done and the privilege of performance which lies ahead.

Efforts should be made to start with a seven-thirty curtain, and only costumes which are involved in quick changes or are other than modern dress need to be used. Time can be saved by using only the character make-ups and limiting the time between scenes to that actually needed for scene or property changes. The director reviews his critique of the night before and checks the play for the last time from the auditorium. The curtain calls are taken through and the director calls the company for the final critique. Actors need to be reminded not to take any wardrobe away from the theatre and asked to be at the theatre by seven P.M. on performance nights or, if they are not, to report in by telephone and explain the delay. It is well to advise that on opening night and during all performances, no visitors will be allowed backstage until the last curtain is down. With a request that all players read through their lines during the next day, the director dismisses the company from the final dress rehearsal.

A distraction important to avoid during the dress rehearsals is the taking of photographs. To keep a cast away from the important business at hand for the sake of a few pictures is unfair. News shots for press use can be taken a week before the opening, using substitute backgrounds if necessary. Photos for the group's permanent record are best taken before performances after the opening. With the play running, the cast will not mind an early call one night for photographs.

On opening night, it is well for the stage managers and crew heads to double check every technical detail well in advance of curtain time. Furniture positions are marked in colored chalk, using different colors for each scene. When there is more than one setting, the exact positions of each flat are marked, at the corners, on the stage floor or ground cloth. The electricians should check all units a half hour before curtain so that any replacement will not be a last minute affair. Sound systems, bells, and all mechanical effects have to be carefully checked before every performance.

For the actors there is also a series of check points. All costumes should be looked over to be certain they are in proper sequence and that all the accessories are present. Personal properties need to be in the exact locations and in sufficient supply. Perhaps all directors know that in the case of small props—the note under the sofa pillow, the calling card or matches in the pocket, the important document in the desk or briefcase—it is prudent to have a duplicate. When items can be lost or covered up in the action of the play, it gives players comfort to know that there is a reserve prop at hand.

Enveloping all this activity is the fine excitement of opening night, a charged atmosphere unique to theatre. It has little to do with nervousness, for our company is prepared; it is, rather, an exhilaration which comes from eagerness to begin. This group of people who were, some of them, strangers to each other at the first tryouts some six weeks ago, have worked into a cohesive, precise team. From their two preview audience experiences they know what a solid foundation is provided by the steps of technique. In the auditorium are gathering the fortunate persons who are going to share the play. For two hours they will forget the realities and difficulties of their own lives and become part of the world on stage. When they leave the theatre they will not be the same as when they came in. Each experience changes a human being, and the condensed emotional span of a play brings laughter or tears or thoughts that might take years of ordinary living to equal.

For the audience, there is refreshment of the spirit; for the actors, the high joy of creativity; for the community, the gain of quality in the civic structure. A group project of the highest order, it occurs tens of thousands of times a year in the United States.

With humility, we know that the quality of the American theatre is far from its zenith. If each generation of those who make theatre can raise that quality even slightly, it will be an important contribution to the sum total of American culture. This worthy objective is possible if we work to recognize and accept the discipline of theatre, including in our efforts sincerity and dignity.

INDEX